What People Are Saying About
The Wellness-Recovery Connection . . .

"Dr. Newport's enthusiasm for wellness and recovery is highly infectious. I especially like the way the book is laid out to provide practical, step-by-step guidance for recovering alcoholics and addicts on how to develop your personalized 'wellness and longevity blueprint' and adopt a wellness lifestyle that is fully compatible with sound principles of recovery and relapse prevention. *The Wellness-Recovery Connection* should serve as a valuable aid for people at all stages of recovery, in embracing a healthy lifestyle that goes hand in hand with enjoying high quality sobriety."

Terence T. Gorski, director, Center for Applied Sciences (CENAPS)
author, *Passages Through Recovery* and coauthor,
Counseling for Relapse Prevention

"*The Wellness-Recovery Connection* will change lives. It is the most comprehensive book ever written on the important issues of health and well-being as they affect recovering people. Author John Newport brings a wealth of knowledge and experience to the topic, and presents this critical information with clarity and grace. This book should be read by all recovering people—and their families."

Jeff Jay, coauthor, *Love First: A New Approach to Intervention for Alcoholism and Drug Addiction*

"*The Wellness-Recovery Connection* is a sweet breath of fresh air. At last, the all-important role of wellness in relapse prevention is elucidated clearly in this well-written and easy-to-use interactive work. In a simple-to-understand fashion Dr. Newport extends the spiritual principles of 12-step programs to their natural conclusion—the wellness lifestyle through which one's spiritual potential can be realized in everyday living."

Emmett E. Miller, M.D., author, *Deep Healing* and
the *Deep Healing* CD, video and cassette series

W9-AGU-848

"*The Wellness-Recovery Connection* is a 'must-read' for persons struggling with chemical dependency and their families, as well as for clinicians who counsel them. Dr. Newport's writing style makes this book a fast read, and it covers a vast number of topics in a simple, easy-to-read manner."

Dianne Wright, MS, RSW, former regional vice president of National Association of Alcoholism and Drug Abuse Counselors (NAADAC) and past president of Michigan Association of Alcoholism and Drug Abuse Counselors (MAADAC)

"As founder of Sierra Tucson, I have dedicated a major portion of my life to addressing wellness in recovery. I applaud Dr. Newport's efforts to bring this information to critical target audiences, namely people in recovery and family members, as well as treatment professionals. *The Wellness-Recovery Connection* is an excellent guide for those who want to strengthen their well-being in sobriety and in life."

William T. O'Donnell Jr.
founder, Sierra Tucson
Tucson, Arizona

"This important, easy-to-use book focuses on wellness as an essential component of recovery from addiction. Put this book to work in your life and you will begin to experience the full joy of sobriety."

William Glasser, M.D., author, *Positive Addiction* and *Warning: Psychiatry Can Be Hazardous to Your Mental Health*

"Trying to recover from alcohol and drug addiction without the tools of wellness is like fighting with one hand tied behind your back. Yet is astonishing how the many dimensions of wellness are often neglected in the treatment field. *The Wellness-Recovery Connection* corrects this oversight, and in doing so brings recovery within the reach of many more people."

Larry Dossey, M.D., author, *Healing Beyond the Body, Reinventing Medicine* and *Healing Words*

"I would highly recommend *The Wellness-Recovery Connection* to anyone in recovery. Dr. Newport's underlying message concerning the importance of healthy lifestyles is extremely important to anyone working a 12-step program. His book provides excellent tools for preventing relapse, as well as for dramatically improving the quality of your life."

Susan Laufer, publisher, *Steps for Recovery*

"*The Wellness-Recovery Connection* is an important book that should be a part of any clinician's therapeutic approach to alcoholism and drug addiction."

Joseph Beasley, M.D., coauthor, *Food for Recovery: The Complete Nutritional Companion for Recovering from Alcoholism, Drug Addiction and Eating Disorders,* director, Addiction End Institute and former department chair, Harvard School of Public Health

THE Wellness-Recovery CONNECTION

Charting Your Pathway to
Optimal Health While Recovering
from Alcoholism and Drug Addiction

John Newport, Ph.D.

Foreword by Terence Gorski

Health Communications, Inc.
Deerfield Beach, Florida

www.hci-online.com

Volume discounts are available for treatment centers and counseling professionals. Please contact Health Communications, Inc., at: (800) 441-5569.

Library of Congress Cataloging-in-Publication Data

Newport, John, 1941-
    The wellness-recovery connection : charting your pathway to optimal health while recovering from alcoholism and drug addiction / John Newport ; foreword by Terence Gorski.
        p. cm.
    ISBN 0-7573-0213-0
    1.   Narcotic   addicts—Rehabilitation. 2.   Alcoholics—Rehabilitation.
3. Substance abuse—Relapse—Prevention. 4. Alcoholism—Relapse—Prevention.
5. Health. I. Title.

RC564.N495 2004
616.86'06—dc22

                                                                    200404239

©2004 John Newport, Ph.D.

ISBN 0-7573-0213-0

Publisher: Health Communications, Inc.
            3201 S.W. 15th Street
            Deerfield Beach, FL 33442–8190

Cover design by Larissa Hise Henoch
Inside book design by Lawna Patterson Oldfield

This book is dedicated to

the many treatment professionals

I have had the privilege of working with

and to the many persons in recovery who have

influenced my life through the positive examples

they model. It is especially dedicated to

Jay and to Charlie, who continue to be

ongoing sources of inspiration.

Contents

Part I: The Importance of Wellness to Recovery

Part II: Integrating the Cornerstones of Wellness into Your Recovery Program

Part III: Your Personal Blueprint for Wellness and Recovery

Foreword

I have specialized in the treatment of addiction and related health-care problems since September 1969. During that time I have come to appreciate the complexity of factors that increase the risk of developing addiction, interfere with early identification and treatment, and cause serious problems with relapse. It has become clear to me that addiction is a life-threatening disease. Attaining meaningful sobriety, therefore, is a lifelong process of successively working though the progressive stages of recovery. In its essence, sobriety is living a meaningful and comfortable life without the need for alcohol or other mood-altering drugs. Yet true sobriety is far more than just healing the damage caused by addiction. Recovery means embracing a lifestyle that promotes continued physical, psychological, social, and spiritual health and growth.

Recovery from chemical dependency is a developmental process that involves successfully navigating a series of progressive stages of recovery. The process of recovery forces us to keep growing, learning and changing. As we move through the early, middle and later stages of recovery, we are constantly challenged to stretch our boundaries and strive for new areas of growth and maturity at all levels of our lives. While recovery is a long-term process that is far from easy, we can learn to enjoy the journey.

I believe that *The Wellness-Recovery Connection* will serve as a valuable resource for persons at all stages of recovery, as well as for their families and treatment professionals. This book is an especially valuable resource for persons in the middle and later stages of recovery, whose growth in their recovery process is appropriately focused on developing a balanced lifestyle, pursuing new horizons of personal growth and enjoying a high-quality sobriety experience.

I firmly agree with Dr. Newport that far too many people in recovery needlessly shortchange themselves of years, even decades, of joyful and productive living by failing to fully embrace a health-conducive lifestyle and incorporate this into their recovery programs. *The Wellness-Recovery Connection* is designed to give you the tools to include a wellness-oriented lifestyle in your recovery program, and to guide you through the process. The points presented throughout this book are fully compatible with 12-step principles.

I especially like the way Dr. Newport has laid out the book to provide practical, step-by-step guidelines for the recovering alcoholic/addict on how to develop a personalized "wellness and longevity blueprint," and adopt a healthy lifestyle that is fully compatible with sound principles of recovery and relapse prevention. Equally important, the book brings a refreshing perspective to bear on the important personal growth aspects of wellness and recovery, including finding and manifesting your central purpose in life, spirituality and life satisfaction.

In reading this book, you will find that Dr. Newport's enthusiasm for wellness and recovery is highly infectious. In summary, *The Wellness-Recovery Connection* should serve as a valuable aid for persons at all stages of recovery, in embracing a healthy lifestyle that goes hand in hand with enjoying high-quality sobriety.

Terence T. Gorski

Terence T. Gorski is founder and director of the Center for Applied Sciences (CENAPS), an addictions training and consulting firm dedicated to providing advanced skills training for addictions professionals, with special emphasis on preventing relapse and assisting persons in recovery in achieving lifelong growth throughout the recovery process. He is the author of *Passages Through Recovery* and coauthor of *Counseling for Relapse Prevention*.

Acknowledgments

I wish to acknowledge the many friends and associates who have contributed to this project through their support and encouragement, as well as through the inspiration and assistance they have graciously provided.

My deepest debt of gratitude is to my wife, Ann, whose heartfelt support and encouragement has been my "guiding light" throughout this entire project.

I especially appreciate Terence Gorski's contribution to this effort through writing the foreword and serving as a constant source of inspiration through his trailblazing work in the field of relapse prevention. I am particularly grateful to Jeff Jay, author of *Love First,* for his constant support and encouragement as my mentor in shepherding this project to publication. I also owe a special vote of thanks to Dianne Wright, former regional vice president of the National Association of Alcoholism and Drug Abuse Counselors and past president of the Michigan Association of Alcoholism and Drug Abuse Counselors, who has provided a steady stream of encouragement throughout the entire project, and who graciously lent her efforts to opening many doors to guide this undertaking to successful completion.

As an author, I have been blessed with a dynamite team that has worked together to move this project forward. Foremost among these are my agent, Rita Rosenkranz, and my editor with HCI Books, Allison Janse. As editor, Allison embraced this project and on many occasions went far beyond the call of duty by offering extremely perceptive insights regarding steps that needed to be taken to bring across the book's essential message with maximum impact. I am also grateful for the contributions of our production editor, Nancy Burke, in further fine-tuning the manuscript. I also wish to acknowledge the contributions of Lucy Wilhelm-Loder (my best friend's sister) in formatting the illustrations.

In reference to the research that forms the basis for many of the ideas presented in this book, I am particularly indebted to Dr. Nancy Jones, my dissertation advisor and dean of the School of Behavioral Science at California Coast University, together with the staff at the Cornerstone Treatment Center in Tustin, California, who tirelessly assisted me in the data collection process. I am especially grateful for the efforts of Michael Stone, M.D., director of Cornerstone; Linda Klinger, administrator; and John Patty, senior counselor. I am also indebted to Jill Brandenberger, R.N., who served as my mentor during my early days in the chemical dependency field and provided valuable input in reference to the study design, and to Nancy Berman, Ph.D., who provided valuable technical assistance in analyzing the study data.

I also would like to acknowledge the special support and encouragement that many friends, family members and associates have generously provided. These special members of my support system include my five grown stepchildren—David, Janice, Linda, Stephen and Laura—and Steven Farmer, Rick MacMahon, Lori Drummond, Susan Laufer, publisher of *Steps for Recovery,* together with Rebecca Hyatt and many other good friends from the Inland Empire Chapter of the Employee Assistance Professionals Association.

I also wish to convey my special thanks to my many "wellness mentors" who have inspired me along my own journey in pursuit of high-level wellness over the past three decades. These include John Travis, Don Ardell, Ken Pelletier, Norman Sheeley, Andrew Weil, Deepak Chopra, Emmett Miller, Larry Dossey, Dean Ornish and Dave Koz (my favorite jazz disc jockey), among others. Finally, I owe a special debt of gratitude to the many addictions treatment professionals and members of the 12-step community with whom I have worked over the years and who serve as a constant source of inspiration.

Introduction

If you are one of the millions of people in active recovery from alcoholism or drug addiction, working your program one day at a time, this book will show you how to enrich your recovery by adopting a wellness lifestyle and reaping the resultant benefits of increased energy and alertness, freedom from illness and a dramatic increase in your overall enjoyment of life. You will also be given the tools to add years—even decades—to your life expectancy.

If you are in the early stages of recovery from an addictive disorder, or if you are a practicing alcoholic/addict who has not yet initiated a recovery program, this book will pinpoint how a wellness-oriented lifestyle can ease the pain of withdrawal and help you over the bumps of the first few months of sobriety while you follow your chosen recovery program. This book will also provide you with valuable pointers concerning how a wellness lifestyle can help you prevent relapse, enabling you to focus your energy on effectively working your recovery program on a day-to-day basis.

If you are the spouse, sibling or child of someone in recovery from alcohol or drug addiction—or if you are in a close relationship with someone who is struggling with addiction—this book is also for you. In her landmark book *Codependent No More,* Melody Beattie vividly describes how spouses and significant others involved with chemically dependent people often suffer serious health consequences. These include heart disease, stomach ulcers, hypertension and other serious illnesses, and are an unintended consequence of constantly picking up the slack for the alcoholic/addict in their lives. If you are closely involved with someone who is either a practicing alcoholic or addict, or is in the process of recovery, this book will provide you with a sound foundation for taking better care of yourself by living well. You can also encourage the recovering alcoholic/addict in your life to follow the guidelines presented in this book. These guidelines can add an exciting new dimension to recovery that promises to dramatically improve the quality of his or her life.

If you are working in the addictions field as a treatment professional, this book will help you assist your clients in their recovery process. It will also give you valuable tools for combating burnout and taking better care of yourself. Sadly, many treatment professionals suffer from a variety of lifestyle imbalances, including nicotine and caffeine addiction, obesity, lack of exercise, inability to manage day-to-day stresses effectively and compulsive workaholism. If you see yourself falling into any of these categories, this book will provide you with invaluable guidance for taking charge of your own health. This, in turn, will enable you to serve as a more effective role model for your clients.

The Wellness-Recovery Connection is an outgrowth of my experience working in the wellness and addictions fields as a treatment program coordinator, counselor and health promotion specialist, together with the research focus of my doctoral studies in psychology. The latter examined the connection between a wellness-oriented lifestyle and success in recovery from alcoholism and drug addiction. My own research, combined with numerous other studies that document the positive benefits to recovery associated with a wellness lifestyle, provide testimony to the existence of a powerful connection between living well and successful sobriety maintenance. This book will provide you with dynamic tools for strengthening your recovery. You will learn how to prevent relapse by stabilizing your brain chemistry, manage daily stresses better, and develop a strong physical constitution and emotional resiliency that will help you weather the ups and downs associated with living clean and sober.

In many places throughout the book, I refer to principles and terminology employed in Alcoholics Anonymous and other 12-step programs. I do so because these programs have guided millions of people to successful recovery, and I have personally witnessed their powerful healing impact on members of my immediate family. By the same token, this book is also intended to be fully compatible with other orientations to recovery that depart from the 12-step model. The important point is to find whatever program works best for you and follow that path.

Sadly, through my work in the addictions field, I have observed that far too many recovering alcoholics and addicts unwittingly end up sabotaging their recovery and shaving years—often decades—off their lives by succumbing to nicotine addiction, compulsive overeating and other self-destructive lifestyle patterns that they unintentionally carry over into their recovery. Happily, you can successfully intervene to break this cycle by following the guidelines presented in this book. It is my earnest hope that you will be motivated to incorporate a new and exciting dimension into your own recovery process through embracing a wellness-oriented lifestyle and charting your pathway to optimal health and personal fulfillment. To your health!

Part One

The Importance of Wellness to Recovery

CHAPTER

1

Wellness:
The Missing Dimension
in Recovery

As you may be aware, you are not the only one who has ever hidden empty wine bottles from your spouse, missed out on a good job due to failing a drug screening or fallen into a pattern of constantly covering up for the irresponsible behavior of an alcoholic spouse or partner. An estimated 5 to 10 percent of Americans are addicted to alcohol and/or other drugs, and patterns of multiple substance abuse are now the norm. Untreated chemical dependency is a major contributing factor to child and spousal abuse, family breakups, unemployment and traffic fatalities—the leading cause of death for people under age twenty-five.

Unfortunately, alcoholics and addicts whose diseases go untreated also eventually suffer major health consequences—including severe damage to their livers, hearts and other vital organs—and often die decades before their time. What you may not be aware of is the fact that millions of people in recovery—perhaps the majority—also shortchange themselves of years of joyful living as a direct result of nicotine addiction, compulsive overeating, junk food addiction and/or other self-destructive behaviors they carry with them into recovery. If you are currently suffering from these or other toxic behavior patterns, you may have acquired these habits as a substitute for your primary addiction to drugs and alcohol. Fortunately, you can free yourself from this vicious cycle—and this book will show you how.

Like most people recovering from addictive disorders, you will need to focus your energy and be disciplined about repairing the damage that years of excessive drinking and drugging have done to your body. As part of a holistic approach to recovery, you must also work on releasing the "baggage" associated with self-defeating mind-sets and behaviors. Instead, you will need to replace that baggage with a life-affirming belief system and a health-conducive lifestyle that fully support your goals in recovery. The good news is that embracing a wellness-oriented lifestyle and working your recovery program go hand in hand.

In his classic bestseller *Positive Addiction,* psychiatrist William Glasser expounds on the benefits associated with replacing negative addictions, or ingrained self-destructive behaviors, with "positive addictions." Examples of positive addictions include regular physical exercise, yoga or meditation, developing an artistic talent, or pursuing a fulfilling hobby. In contrast to negative addictions, such as alcohol or drug addiction, which tend to foster unhealthy dependencies and decreased self-esteem, positive addictions contribute to improved quality of life, heightened self-esteem and increased feelings of independence. One of

Glasser's key points is that positive addictions are very effective tools for freeing ourselves from the grips of our negative addictions.

In this book, you will learn about the numerous positive addictions associated with a wellness-oriented lifestyle and how to embrace them as integral components of a truly holistic approach to recovery. Equally important, you will learn to appreciate how a healthy lifestyle can help you successfully navigate the various stages of recovery and safeguard against relapse.

The Importance of Wellness to Your Recovery

If you completed a chemical dependency treatment program, you most likely learned about the benefits of physical exercise and sound nutrition in repairing the damage done to your body by excessive use of alcohol and drugs. You probably also received an introduction to the importance of basic stress management skills in maintaining day-to-day sobriety and guarding against relapse.

Primary treatment, or the initial phase of treatment, generally focuses some attention on basic wellness concepts. Unfortunately, these concepts often receive less than adequate attention during the critically important, yet oft-neglected continuing care phase of treatment. This sad state of affairs is a reflection of what I call the neglected stepchild syndrome. In today's health-care environment, with its overriding emphasis on cost containment, mental health services have become the neglected stepchild of medical care. Chemical dependency treatment has become the neglected stepchild of mental health, and continuing care, which should form the cornerstone of ongoing recovery maintenance, tends to be severely shortchanged.

Another reason wellness lifestyles often receive less than adequate emphasis in treatment stems from the failure of many treatment professionals to take good care of themselves. Far too many treatment professionals suffer from a variety of lifestyle imbalances, including nicotine and caffeine addiction, obesity, lack of exercise and compulsive workaholism. As such, they are in a poor position to serve as role models in motivating their clients to adopt wellness-oriented lifestyles.

Yet another obstacle to living well stems from the conflicting demands and time pressures that all of us experience in today's fast-paced society. In recovery, we often feel overwhelmed by the overlapping demands of earning a living, engaging in family life, going to meetings, studying the steps and doing the million and one other things that creep into our overly crowded lives. In the context of such a pressure-cooker environment, our well-intentioned plans to launch an exercise program, bring our diet into balance, give up smoking or take up meditation all too often fail to materialize.

As you can see, many influences conspire to work against our devoting appropriate attention to living healthy during recovery. The net result is that millions of people in recovery neglect this critically important area. Predictably, they end up paying the price in terms of unwittingly setting themselves up for relapse, as well as for heart disease, emphysema, various forms of cancer and a host of other devastating illnesses that can often be prevented.

The good news is that you have a choice. In many respects, by virtue of demonstrating the courage and commitment that has taken you this far in working your recovery program, you have a leg up on most Americans in terms of embracing a healthy lifestyle. Just as you have learned to work your core recovery program step by step, you can likewise learn to embrace a wellness-oriented lifestyle and effectively integrate it into your recovery program—simply by taking "one step at a time."

Wellness Defined

Wellness can be defined as the dynamic process of taking charge of your health and programming yourself to attain optimal health and well-being. As this book demonstrates, you are in the driver's seat. You set your own goals and priorities, design and implement your wellness program, and determine how far you want to go toward claiming your birthright to optimal health, longevity and self-fulfillment.

You are about to embark on an exciting journey that will truly transform your life. In a nutshell, this book will show you how to:

- Supercharge your recovery by integrating a wellness-oriented lifestyle into your 12-step program.
- Inventory your strengths and weaknesses regarding health and wellness, with particular reference to lifestyle influences.
- Identify the wellness goals that are most important to you—including your optimum life expectancy and the immediate wellness benefits you would like to enjoy—and implement an action plan for achieving these goals.
- Launch your personal quest for uncovering and expressing your unique sense of purpose in life—zeroing in on those

core values and goals that are truly important to you—and channeling your focused energy into transforming your dreams into reality.

- Gain increased self-esteem, energy, alertness and confidence as you pursue your pathway to greater health.
- Learn how taking care of yourself will enable you to give much more to your friends, family and other people in recovery!

2

The Importance of Wellness to Early Recovery and Relapse Prevention

In keeping with the basic 12-step principle "first things first," let's look at how you can use the tools of wellness to successfully navigate the treacherous waters of early recovery. Then we will look at how the many benefits associated with a wellness lifestyle can actively help safeguard you against relapse.

The Acute Withdrawal Process

If you are currently in recovery from alcoholism and/or drug addiction, you are intimately familiar with the range of uncomfortable symptoms associated with acute withdrawal. In reference to alcohol withdrawal, acute withdrawal symptoms typically begin when the blood alcohol concentration declines sharply—generally within four to twelve hours after alcohol use has been discontinued. The acute withdrawal process typically runs its course over four to seven days. Throughout this period, the process of detoxifying your body is about as much fun as a root canal and IRS audit combined! By way of quick review, the following symptoms are generally associated with acute withdrawal:

- Sweating combined with tachycardia, or elevated heart rate
- Hand tremors
- Insomnia
- Nausea and/or vomiting
- Anxiety, often accompanied by depression

In rare situations, visual, auditory or tactile hallucinations and grand mal seizures may also accompany the acute withdrawal process.

If you are actively drinking or drugging and feel that you are ready to quit, it would probably be advisable to link up with a treatment program to help you overcome the hurdles of acute withdrawal and get you started on the right track. Your local Alcoholics Anonymous (AA) or Narcotics Anonymous (NA) Central Office can refer you to a variety of resources in line with your needs, preferences and financial limitations. If you have been a heavy drinker and/or drug user for over ten years, or if you are aware of any significant medical conditions that may complicate your withdrawal process, you may want to consider undergoing medically supervised detoxification.

Let's now look at how wellness tools can help you during acute withdrawal and early recovery.

Using Wellness Tools to Help You Through
Acute Withdrawal and Early Recovery

- Ease your way over the humps of acute withdrawal by practicing deep breathing, listening to relaxation tapes and using other stress-management techniques.
- Reduce your cravings for addictive drugs by curbing your intake of caffeine and sugar—as well as by snacking on fresh fruits, veggies and other nutritious foods when cravings strike.
- Use nutritional supplements to help vitalize your bodily systems during detoxification, as well as during the post-acute withdrawal period of recovery. (Check with a physician or a nutritionist specializing in addictions for an appropriate vitamin/mineral/herbal formula.)
- Go for a jog, a fast walk or partake in any other form of vigorous exercise to stimulate the production of endorphins—giving you a totally free natural high!
- Begin to normalize your sleeping patterns by listening to relaxation tapes at bedtime or practicing self-hypnosis. (Also, try listening to relaxing music while taking a hot bath right before bedtime.)
- Use the wellness tools presented in this book—including exercise, learning to eat well, and meditation/other stress management tools—as *effective substitutes* for drinking and drugging. These will give you a helpful "boost" during early recovery through contributing to increased vitality and self-esteem.
- Learn to focus on your *unique purpose* for being on this planet—which will give you a powerful incentive for not returning to drinking and drugging! (More on this in chapter 9.)

Wellness Tools

Let's take a few moments to focus more specifically on some of the ways in which wellness tools can help smooth the transition through detoxification and the early stages of recovery. Using the deep breathing exercises, meditation and the other stress management techniques described in chapter 7 can help you counteract the blahs and anxiety associated with acute withdrawal. They can also act as coping tools that may help safeguard you against relapse.

Chapters 4 and 5 will provide you with more details concerning the important role of sound nutrition in providing a solid biochemical foundation for your lifelong recovery process. During early recovery, you can effectively counteract the cravings for addictive substances by curbing your intake of caffeine and sugar, as well as by snacking on nutritious foods when cravings strike. Healthy "craving-busters" include carrot sticks, fresh or dried fruit and nuts. I also strongly recommend that you consider strengthening your system by making judicious use of nutritional supplements during the withdrawal and early recovery periods. Rather than self-prescribing, please consult a physician, naturopath or nutritionist with special training in addictive disorders to help you zero in on a vitamin/mineral/herbal formula that is most appropriate to your special needs.

Incidentally, if you are newly sober and attending meetings of AA, NA or any other recovery-focused support group, you may encounter "old-timers" guzzling coffee and eating candy bars, and encouraging you to do the same. From a wellness perspective, I do believe it's best to ease up on the caffeine and sugar during early sobriety. While you may choose to disagree with some of the "old-timers" in terms of their affinity for caffeine and sugar, don't let this blindside you to the wisdom they can impart in other areas relating to successful sobriety.

Very often, the body's ability to produce endorphins—those lovely natural chemicals that trigger the pleasure centers of the brain—is impaired during the early stages of recovery. This can be particularly true if you are coming down from cocaine, amphetamines or other stimulants. You can help your body get back into full gear in the endorphin-production department by engaging in jogging, fast walking and other forms of vigorous exercise. (The role of exercise in wellness and recovery is discussed more fully in chapter 6.) It is also important to note that the wellness tools presented in this book—including exercise, learning to eat well and the various stress management techniques—work in synergistic fashion as effective substitutes for drinking and drugging.

You also need to take steps to normalize your sleeping patterns, which are typically disrupted during the early months of recovery. The deep breathing and self-hypnosis exercises presented below are designed to help you maximize your experience of serenity during the early months of recovery.

Stress-Buster Deep Breathing Exercise

One of the reasons Americans are so stressed out is that we are a nation of shallow breathers. The purpose of this exercise is to increase the flow of oxygen to your brain and body, simultaneously calming and energizing you. You can do this exercise either standing or sitting upright.

Place your left hand over your navel above your stomach and your right hand on your chest. Breathe in while slowly counting to four, and breathe out while counting to eight.

KEY: Focus on breathing from the bottom up—that is, on filling your lungs from the bottom to the top. You should feel your stomach moving in and out as you inhale and exhale, but feel little movement in your chest.

"Belly breathe" for a minute or two twice a day, or whenever you begin to feel overly stressed.

A Gentle Breathing Exercise for Relaxation

Try this exercise whenever you feel a need to be more calm and centered.

Place your hand over your navel and gently inhale, silently saying "I am" as you fill your chest.

As you exhale, silently say "relaxed."

Repeat this gentle breathing process for a minute or two, allowing your breathing to gently relax you and bring you back to center.

A Simple Self-Hypnosis Exercise to Ease You into Relaxing Sleep

1. Note: You may find it helpful to tape-record this exercise and listen to it as you lie in bed preparing for sleep. Lie in bed with your eyes closed and focus your attention on your breathing. Become aware of the gentle rhythm of breathing in (taking in rich, fresh oxygen) and breathing out (releasing accumulated toxins along with your breath). Take several slow, deep breaths and experience yourself sinking into deeper relaxation with each breath.

2. Imagine that you are at the top of a stairway and slowly descending, counting down from twenty to one. Count down slowly, and allow yourself to feel more and more deeply relaxed with each downward step. (You may find that you drift off to sleep before you get down to the bottom of the staircase!)

3. At the bottom of the stairway, visualize yourself entering your own very special place of peace and relaxation. This might be a quiet beach, a lake high up in the mountains or perhaps a special place associated with your childhood. It really doesn't matter, as long as you choose a place of serenity and relaxation that holds special meaning for you.

4. Allow yourself to fully experience your special place's environment, noticing the temperature and other weather conditions, whether you are indoors or outdoors, the time of day, etc.

5. As you are experiencing the serenity of your special place, say a silent prayer to your higher power and turn over to him or her any distressing thoughts or feelings you may be carrying with you. Completely release them to your higher power for safekeeping. You may also want to visualize these thoughts and feelings as helium-filled balloons that are drifting away, up into the sky, millions and millions of miles away.

6. Close your prayer by asking your higher power to guide you gently to a peaceful and relaxing sleep, so that you can begin the new day totally refreshed and energized.

Note: If you awaken during the night, simply repeat this exercise. With practice, it will become easier and easier to return to a deep and restful sleep.

Role of Wellness in Relapse Prevention

Relapse—the return to former patterns of addictive behavior—is the most frightening word in any recovering person's vocabulary. The prospect of relapse is doubly frightening if you are the recovering person's spouse. Invariably, you feel completely helpless and devastated when your partner falls off the wagon despite your best efforts to support his or her recovery process. This section focuses on action steps that you, the person in recovery, can take to minimize your personal risk of relapse, together with how a wellness lifestyle can assist you in that process.

First the Bad News

In reality, many recovering alcoholics and addicts relapse several times before achieving long-term sobriety. Follow-up studies consistently show that the rate of relapse following treatment is disturbingly high. Some studies report that 80 to 90 percent of alcoholics and addicts succumb to relapse, sometimes years after initiating their recovery process.

The recovery-relapse cycle becomes a vicious roller-coaster ride for far too many recovering people and their families—turning their lives completely upside down. As you may have experienced yourself, adverse consequences of relapse can include:

- Weakening of family ties due to erosion of trust as family members are let down again.
- Shattering of the recovering person's self-esteem and reinforcement of a negative self-image as a "hopeless failure."
- Loss of gainful employment and financial ruin.
- Domestic violence and family breakups.

• Devastation of the alcoholic/addict's health due to resumption of abusive drinking and drug use.

The 1989 *Exxon Valdez* oil spill provides a chilling example of the heavy damage associated with relapse. This ecological tragedy, which caused severe damage to Alaska's coastline, resulted in court-imposed damages against Exxon of $125 million. Investigations of this incident revealed that the freighter's captain, who had previously completed alcoholism treatment, had been seen drinking the day before the spill.

When are you, as a recovering alcoholic/addict, at greatest risk of succumbing to relapse? Terence Gorski, a leading authority in relapse prevention, states that recovering people are particularly vulnerable to relapse during the early stages of recovery. Many, if not most, relapses occur during what is called the post-acute withdrawal period, which typically runs anywhere from six months to up to two years following detoxification. According to Gorski, post-acute withdrawal is a physiological and neurological adjustment process that the body goes through in response to discontinuing use of addictive substances, following years of abusive drinking or drug usage. Brain functioning is affected during this adjustment process, with spells of confusion, difficulty in concentration and increased vulnerability to stressful situations.

Normally, post-acute withdrawal symptoms will subside as a result of the body's natural healing processes, which can take anywhere from six months to two years to run their course. During this period, as a recovering person you tend to be particularly vulnerable to relapse, especially if you are unaware of the dynamics associated with post-acute withdrawal. If you are attempting to navigate this vulnerable period in early recovery, you may want to copy the chart on page 20 and carry it with you as a reminder of the powerful tools that a wellness lifestyle provides you.

In addition to your heightened susceptibility to relapse during early recovery, you are also at risk at any point in your life when you encounter high-risk factors that act as "trigger points" and target your greatest areas of vulnerability. Examples of high-risk situations that can trigger a relapse include:

- loss of a job
- excessive family problems (including divorce)
- death of a relative or close friend
- cumulative stress overload caused by juggling too many conflicting demands
- a life-threatening illness
- social pressures to return to drinking and/or drug use

Major catastrophic events can also be associated with increased likelihood of relapse. Terence Gorski reports that the tragic events of September 11, 2001, which claimed the lives of thousands of innocent Americans, were followed by an upward spike in alcohol and drug consumption (including a marked increase in consumption of antianxiety medications). Additionally, treatment centers and addictions professionals across the country reported increased rates of relapse.

Now the Good News

The good news is that relapse is preventable, and a wellness-oriented lifestyle can play a major role in reducing your personal risk of relapse.

In his bestsellers *Passages in Recovery* and *Counseling for Relapse*

Prevention, Terence Gorski emphasizes the importance of developing a personalized relapse prevention strategy, anticipating and tuning in to early warning signs of impending relapse, and involving family members and other key supportive people in your prevention plan. Warning signs of impending relapse often include:

- Increased irritability and strained social relationships
- Irregular eating habits
- Major disruption in sleeping patterns
- Periods of deep depression
- Irregular attendance at 12-step meetings or other recovery support groups
- Feeling overwhelmed by life's pressures
- Entertaining increasing thoughts of drinking and/or drugging as an escape

Significantly, Gorski underscores the critical importance of health-conducive lifestyle changes in relapse prevention, particularly in reference to the post-acute withdrawal process associated with the early stages of recovery. In his words, "[The recovering person] can learn to manage the symptoms of post-acute withdrawal through a program of education, stress management, diet, exercise, relaxation and life-management skills training." In particular, Gorski emphasizes that the relative severity of post-acute withdrawal symptoms tends to increase in direct proportion to the level of stress in the recovering person's life. Hence, any sound lifestyle measures designed to increase your tolerance to stressful situations will yield tangible dividends in terms of relapse prevention.

The following chart highlights how a wellness lifestyle can help you prevent relapse. Study this chart for pointers that you

can incorporate into your own relapse prevention program—we
will "flesh out" the details in the chapters that lie ahead.

As previously mentioned, psychiatrist William Glasser advocates replacing chemical dependency and other negative

---

How Living Well Can Help Prevent Relapse

- Living well will help you manifest a strong sense of purpose in life
  and will reinforce your commitment to clean and sober living.
- You will learn to identify your relapse triggers—and defuse these
  triggers—by acquiring the skills to manage day-to-day stresses
  effectively.
- You will learn how to calm your mind by practicing meditation,
  yoga and/or other stress-reduction techniques. This will help you
  acquire the resiliency you need to deal with the ups and downs of
  living sober.
- Living well will help repair the damage to your central nervous
  system and other bodily systems. This will give you the strength
  and vitality to confront life's challenges "head on," without the
  need for any artificial crutches.
- Through learning how to follow a wholesome, nutritious diet,
  you will be able to combat the biochemical triggers that are frequently associated with relapse.
- As you follow your pathway to optimal health, living well will
  increasingly become a central focus of your life. You'll be having
  so much fun that you will never want to go back to drinking and
  drugging!
- The life-affirming, health-conducive belief system associated with
  living well will enable you to work your recovery program even
  more effectively—providing a powerful safeguard against relapse.

addictions with positive addictions. He defines these as habitual activities that are intrinsically rewarding and serve to bolster your self-esteem. Examples of positive addictions include many of the behaviors associated with a wellness-oriented lifestyle, including running and other vigorous forms of exercise, training for competitive sports, learning a musical instrument, taking up meditation, and engaging in other creative and challenging pursuits.

How does Glasser's concept of "positive addictions" apply to our immediate concern with preventing relapse? In short, to the extent that you are able to replace your former self-destructive behaviors with positive addictions, you are at a substantially reduced risk of relapsing. Working a 12-step program and pursuing a wellness-oriented lifestyle are prime examples of positive addictions that can be intrinsically self-rewarding.

G. Alan Marlatt, director of the Addictive Behaviors Research Center at the University of Washington in Seattle, is an authority on relapse prevention who closely identifies with Glasser's concept of positive addictions. Marlatt advocates a strategic approach to relapse prevention that centers on lifestyle modification, coupled with learning to effectively respond to early warning signs of impending relapse and developing effective coping strategies to employ in high risk situations. According to Marlatt, a health-conducive lifestyle is an important component of an effective relapse prevention strategy because it provides a battery of lifestyle coping skills that foster improved physical, psychological and spiritual well-being. Simultaneously, this lifestyle also bolsters the recovering person's self-esteem and enables them to deal with high-risk situations or relapse triggers more effectively.

Sounds Great, But Does It Really Work?

In short, yes. However, if you or your partner have gone through the roller-coaster ride of treatment, relapse and resumption of treatment time and time again, you may be understandably skeptical of yet another approach that promises success provided you "work the program." Fortunately, there is a growing body of research that focuses on whether the various shifts in behavior associated with a wellness-oriented lifestyle are, in fact, associated with reduced risk of relapse.

A classic study based in Canada focused on the effects of a physical conditioning program among subjects completing residential treatment for alcoholism. Fifty-eight subjects who underwent a daily conditioning program—consisting of one hour of progressively vigorous physical activity over the course of the six weeks—were compared with two groups of subjects who completed the treatment program without the exercise component. At the end of three months, following completion of treatment, all three groups were surveyed concerning whether they successfully maintained abstinence from drinking.

Significantly, the reported rate of abstinence among subjects participating in the fitness program (69.3 percent) was almost twice as high as the abstinence rate for subjects in the two control groups (38.0 percent and 36.9 percent, respectively).

As we will discuss more fully in chapter 7, learning and practicing effective stress-reduction techniques is also associated with reduced risk of relapse. In the early 1990s, a group of researchers conducted a comparative analysis of twenty-four studies focusing on the impact of daily meditation practice—a frequently advocated stress-management technique—on participants' alcohol and drug consumption. Findings of all twenty-four studies indicated significant positive benefits associated with regular practice of meditation in terms of increased abstinence from alcohol and drugs, and reduced incidence of relapse.

My own research, conducted in 1998, focused on examining the association between a wellness-oriented lifestyle and successful recovery, as indicated by freedom from relapse, among a group of fifty multiple substance abusers who had completed residential treatment. Study subjects were equally divided into two groups—the successful recovery group, who completed treatment and maintained sobriety for at least six months, and the relapse group, who completed treatment and subsequently relapsed. Each subject completed a Lifestyle Assessment Questionnaire designed to assess his or her standing in relation to eleven areas generally associated with a wellness-oriented lifestyle:

- level of physical exercise
- stress/stress management
- nutrition/weight control
- social supports
- sleep patterns
- smoking/smoking cessation
- caffeine consumption
- life satisfaction
- overall health status
- perceived control over matters relating to their health
- spirituality

The highest possible "wellness index" score, computed from subjects' questionnaire responses, was 90. The higher the score, the healthier the subject's lifestyle.

As a group, subjects in the recovery group registered significantly higher scores than those in the relapse group. Specifically, the twenty-five subjects in the recovery group registered an average score of 54.8, compared with an average score of only 39.1 for subjects in the relapse group. The likelihood of this association occurring by chance is less than one in 1,000. Furthermore, subjects in the recovery group registered higher average scores for virtually all component items in the wellness index.

Incidentally, while the average score of 54.8 registered by the clean and sober subjects is certainly far from optimal, remember that this represents a randomly chosen group of people who had no access to the wellness pointers presented in this book. The important point is that their scores suggest they were moving in the right direction, while enjoying the benefits of living clean and sober.

In addition to focusing on the subjects' involvement in a wellness-oriented lifestyle, my study also surveyed subjects regarding their participation in 12-step meetings. Significantly, 88 percent of subjects in the recovery group reported that they attended 12-step meetings at least once a week, compared with only 36 percent of subjects in the relapse group. Taken together, these findings suggest that a wellness-oriented lifestyle can be of significant benefit in safeguarding against relapse. These findings also strongly suggest that a wellness-oriented lifestyle and active participation in a 12-step program combine to strengthen your overall sobriety and minimize the prospect of relapse.

In summary, I believe that the following three-pronged strategy provides the best level of protection against relapse for recovering alcoholics/addicts:

- Actively work your chosen recovery program. If you are following a 12-step program, develop an ongoing relationship with your sponsor, go to meetings and work the 12 steps. If you are following a different path, be sure to take full advantage of available support from your chosen program.
- Develop an active relapse prevention strategy. This involves becoming familiar with the personal "trigger points" that heighten your risk of relapse, and implementing effective coping strategies.
- Assign a high priority to taking care of yourself, and actively embrace a wellness-oriented lifestyle. In particular, work on bringing your diet into balance to safeguard against excessive sugar consumption and other nutritional stressors that often trigger relapse. This book will give you the tools to chart your own pathway to optimal health, together with step-by-step guidance for implementing this process.

In addition to helping securely anchor you in your day-to-day sobriety, a wellness lifestyle offers major benefits in terms of enjoying increased health and vitality across the board, together with dramatic improvements in your overall quality of life. This forms the focus of the following chapter.

3

Claiming Your Birthright to Optimal Health

As previously stated, millions of people in recovery unwittingly fail to fully exercise their birthright to optimal health and longevity. Fortunately, this does not need to happen to you. In this chapter I will introduce you to the various dimensions of wellness and discuss their role in taking charge of your health. You will then receive a sneak preview about how to customize the many tools of wellness to supercharge your recovery and reap the exciting benefits associated with a wellness-oriented lifestyle.

Wellness and Longevity: A Current Snapshot

As a society, we have enjoyed an unprecedented increase in average life expectancy over the past century. On the average, an

American child born in 1900 could only expect to live to age forty-nine. By contrast, life expectancy at birth today is seventy-four years for males and eighty years for females. Contributing factors to these dramatic gains include medical advances, improved sanitation and public health measures, and a dramatically increased health consciousness among the public.

Major advances in medical science have included the virtual conquest of smallpox, diphtheria and many other communicable diseases, which were formerly the leading cause of death, together with major inroads in detection and treatment of today's major health challenges, particularly heart disease, cancer and stroke.

Our corresponding progress in terms of incorporating the basic tools of wellness into our lives is, at best, a double-edged sword. On the one hand, our knowledge of lifestyle-associated risk factors linked to many major illnesses, particularly heart disease and cancer, has increased substantially over the past forty years. Consequently, millions of enlightened Americans have taken up exercise, begun to clean up their diets, given up smoking and embraced other healthy lifestyle choices. At the same time, we are seeing some very disturbing trends. According to the national Centers for Disease Control and Prevention, over 30 percent of all adult Americans are now obese (defined as 30 percent or more above their ideal body weight), and close to two-thirds (66 percent) are overweight.

We are suffering from a nationwide epidemic of obesity and sedentary lifestyles. Even more disturbing, in far too many cases this pattern is becoming established at a very early age, with children unwittingly setting themselves up for a lifetime of serious medical problems.

While the overall gains in average life expectancy over the past century are certainly impressive, in my opinion these only represent the tip of the iceberg. I firmly believe that most of us can program ourselves to exceed these averages and enjoy life spans extending into the mideighties, midnineties and beyond, simply by embracing the principles advocated in this book. Taking charge of your health is the key!

Factors Influencing Your State of Health

Presented here is a chart summarizing data from the Centers for Disease Control, entitled "Factors Influencing A Person's Health."

The data presented in this chart is extremely empowering. While we have no control over our choice of parents, the overall influence of heredity on individual wellness—according to the experts—is relatively small. The greater majority of factors influencing our overall health status—a full 84 percent—are ones we can directly control or influence through our lifestyles and personal choices. Significantly, our lifestyle choices—including our choices about exercise, nutrition, managing day-to-day stress, and using alcohol, drugs, nicotine or other toxic substances—account for over 50 percent of the factors influencing our state of health. We can also positively influence many of the environmental factors affecting our daily lives.

Certainly, you cannot expect to make sweeping changes in all of these areas overnight. However, as I will show you in the pages ahead, a personal commitment to positive change in one or more areas can yield dramatic improvements in a relatively short time. The one essential factor on which all actions hinge is motivation.

Factors Influencing a Person's Health

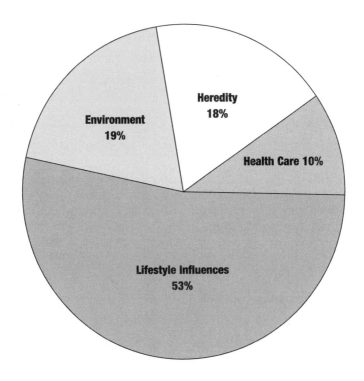

Source: U.S. Centers for Disease Control and Prevention

Dimensions of Wellness

Let's take a closer look at the dimensions of wellness that form the cornerstones of the wellness-oriented lifestyle I am urging you to adopt. On the next page you will find an adaptation of the Wellness-Illness Continuum, originally developed by wellness pioneer Dr. John Travis.

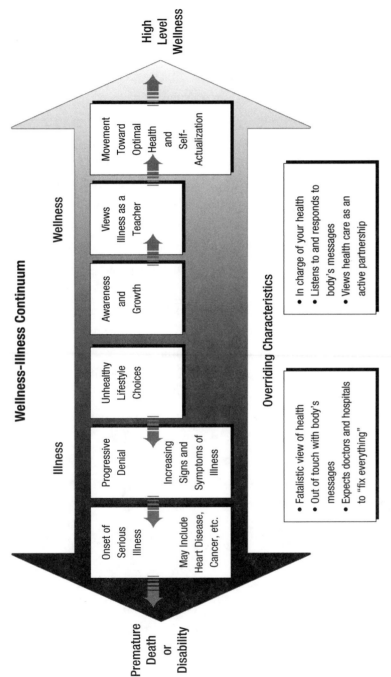

Wellness-Illness Continuum

High Level Wellness

Wellness

Illness

Premature Death or Disability

- Movement Toward Optimal Health and Self-Actualization
- Views Illness as a Teacher
- Awareness and Growth
- Unhealthy Lifestyle Choices
- Progressive Denial / Increasing Signs and Symptoms of Illness
- Onset of Serious Illness / May Include Heart Disease, Cancer, etc.

Overriding Characteristics

- In charge of your health
- Listens to and responds to body's messages
- Views health care as an active partnership

- Fatalistic view of health
- Out of touch with body's messages
- Expects doctors and hospitals to "fix everything"

Adapted from "Illness-Wellness Continuum," originally appearing in *Wellness Workbook* by John W. Travis, M.D., and Regina Sarah Ryan, Ten Speed Press, ©1981, 1988, 2004.

As you can see, the left side of the continuum depicts key characteristics associated with what we might call an illness-oriented lifestyle. The right side illustrates the mind-set and behaviors associated with progressive movement through the wellness side of the continuum.

Most Americans are locked into the illness side of the spectrum, at one level or another. This is especially true with people who are actively engaged in alcoholism, drug addiction and other addictive disorders. When we are "hanging out" on the illness side of the continuum, we tend to drift from various signs and symptoms of impending illness, which are generally minor at first. As these symptoms grow stronger, we then move through a veil of denial that eventually culminates in the development of heart disease, cancer or other serious illness. Typically, this cycle plays itself out over several decades, with the ultimate outcome being either premature death or disability.

As illustrated in the chart, an illness-oriented lifestyle is associated with a fatalistic view of health, being out of touch with our bodies, and by an attitude toward health care in which doctors and hospitals are expected to fix the problem.

In contrast, a lifestyle oriented toward wellness is associated with ever-increasing awareness and growth, together with a progressive movement toward creating optimal health and well-being. Significantly, when you are moving through the wellness side of the continuum, you are striving for self-actualization—that is, you are involved in an ongoing quest to uncover and fully develop your unique potential as a person.

Perhaps most importantly, when you are on the wellness side of the continuum you view yourself as actively in charge of your health. *You* are in the driver's seat! You befriend your body and heed its messages that signal distress and the need for healing at various levels. When you do encounter a challenging illness (which eventually happens to all of us), you make a conscious effort to view that illness as a teacher, asking "What can I learn from this experience?"

On which side of the continuum do you wish to be? The choice is up to you.

Let's move on and examine the various dimensions of wellness. These will serve as a foundation for developing your personal blueprint for high-level wellness as you incorporate the

Dimensions of Wellness

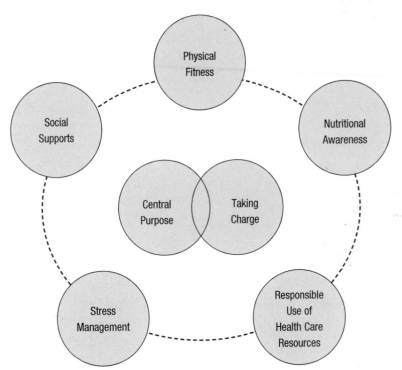

tools presented throughout the book. At the bottom of the preceding page is a diagram I developed to depict some of the essential dimensions of wellness as I currently envision them.

Note that I have depicted the two core dimensions of wellness, *central purpose* and *taking charge,* as overlapping circles. I emphatically believe that finding and manifesting your unique sense of purpose represents the wellspring of optimal health and longevity, from which all else flows. Indeed, I am convinced that it is no coincidence that throughout history, men and women whose lives were marked by a profound sense of purpose have almost universally enjoyed life spans far in excess of those experienced by their contemporaries. When we are truly "doing our thing," we are motivated on both the conscious and subconscious levels to bring our lives into alignment with the governing principles of the universe. Then, and only then, do we experience a profound sense of motivation to take charge of our health.

Revolving around the core dimensions of *central purpose* and *taking charge* of our health are a few of what I like to call the active dimensions of wellness. This diagram is not meant to be exhaustive, and you can no doubt think of other dimensions that are equally worthy of being included. Some of the key active dimensions of wellness that I have identified include:

- Nutritional awareness
- Physical fitness
- Stress management
- Social supports
- Making responsible use of health care resources

In part two of this book we will take a detailed tour of each of these dimensions. You will be given step-by-step guidelines concerning actions you can take to incorporate a particular dimension into your life. In the final chapters, you will receive definitive guidelines for developing and launching your own personal blueprint for wellness and recovery.

Parallels Between Wellness and the 12-Step Recovery Model

There are many parallels between a wellness lifestyle and working a 12-step recovery program. Let's take a moment to highlight some of the striking parallels between pursuing high-level wellness and working a 12-step program.

The Disease Process

As everyone who is working a 12-step recovery program is well aware, a key cornerstone of successful recovery is the recognition that chemical dependency is a disease process that is both progressive and self-destructive in nature.

In a similar vein, the wellness model recognizes that most diseases result from the cumulative impact on our bodies of self-destructive behaviors—behaviors that we can learn to control. Certainly, there is a hereditary component to major illnesses such as heart disease, hypertension, diabetes and cancer. Yet medical science has firmly established that the onset of these progressive conditions, which generally runs a course of several decades, is clearly linked to behavioral patterns that we can learn to change. Common threads running through these self-destructive behaviors include improper diet, lack of exercise, cigarette smoking and the inability to effectively manage day-to-day stresses in our lives.

Personal Responsibility for a Lifelong Growth Process

In both the 12-step and wellness models, the concept of personal responsibility represents the flip side of the disease process, guiding us along the road to recovery. While AA and other 12-step programs maintain that as an alcoholic or addict you are not responsible for your disease, they emphatically urge you to assume personal responsibility for embarking on a lifelong process of recovery.

As stated previously, the basic cornerstone of wellness is taking charge of your health. In the wellness model, you are motivated to assume personal responsibility for your own health and well-being. If you happen to be suffering from heart disease or another serious illness, there are many steps that you can take to start turning the disease process around. In parallel with basic 12-step principles, the wellness model views your personal quest for high-level wellness as a lifelong process of personal growth and discovery.

Spirituality

In all 12-step programs, believing in a power greater than yourself (commonly called a "higher power") is viewed as being essential to recovery. Furthermore, as you work your way through the program, you grow spiritually by seeking to improve your conscious contact with a higher power, and by making amends and reaching out to help other alcoholics and addicts who are still suffering.

I believe there is also an active spiritual core running through the wellness movement. Most wellness advocates view the quest for central purpose in our lives as the wellspring of total health and well-being. Most wellness advocates also subscribe to the view that engaging in positive social action represents a logical extension of our personal commitment to wellness. To cite a personal example: as I have become actively involved in cleaning up my diet and eating lighter on the food chain over the past several decades, I have concurrently experienced a heightened awareness concerning the plight of billions of people on this planet who do not have enough to eat.

As you can see, there are a number of striking parallels between the 12-step principles of recovery and a wellness-oriented lifestyle. This was emphatically brought home to me in my recent research focusing on recovering alcoholics/addicts who had completed residential treatment. One of the most striking findings was that the successful recovery group (defined as participants who had maintained sobriety for six months or longer) not only scored significantly higher on my wellness questionnaire than the subjects who had relapsed, but also regularly attended 12-step meetings at least once a week.

Your Preliminary Wellness Inventory

In chapter 11, you will be asked to complete a detailed wellness assessment and create a set of goals, as part of charting your personal road map to high-level wellness. At this point, however, I would invite you to spend a few minutes on a preliminary wellness inventory, which is designed to help you focus on where you stand right now and where you would like to go. Note that this "mini-inventory" addresses life goals, as well as health status and longevity potential. This is important because from a holistic perspective, wellness is fully concerned with all dimensions of our lives, including the spiritual—over and above the more measurable indicators of health status.

Now, turn to the Preliminary Wellness Inventory at the end of this chapter and answer the questions as honestly as possible. I encourage you to take a pen and paper to jot down your response to each question, and save these notes for future reference.

Taking Charge of Your Health

Earlier in this chapter, we talked about the dramatic gains in life expectancy that Americans have enjoyed over the past century. Despite the impressive statistics among the general population, far too few recovering alcoholics and addicts are sharing in the same overall gains. While "working their programs" and diligently maintaining abstinence from their primary drugs of choice, far too many people in recovery continue to cling to unhealthy lifestyle-related "baggage" associated with their former addictive pursuits.

If you are dragging some of this baggage along with you, don't despair. This book is dedicated to empowering you, as a recovering alcoholic/addict, to *take charge of your health* and reap the full benefits of optimal health, well-being and increased life expectancy.

Focus for a moment on the life goals section of the wellness inventory you just completed. Hopefully you have identified one or more goals that are truly important to you and that will serve to motivate you to focus your energies on creating optimal health and vitality in your life.

Now take a moment to consider your response to question

two—health status. If you rated your overall state of health as good or excellent, then you are already doing some of the right things. This book will reinforce the direction you are moving in and assist you with fine-tuning the process. If you rated your health status as fair or having "lots of room for improvement," you are presumably motivated to make some changes in this area of your life (otherwise you would not have read this far into the book).

Also, reflect on your responses concerning the immediate health benefits associated with a wellness lifestyle that you would like to enjoy. Note that I purposely asked you to focus your attention on the immediate gains that you would like to experience, before asking you to attempt to pinpoint how long you would ideally like to live. If you are feeling fully energized and enjoying life to the fullest—all systems go, so to speak— chances are that you would like to live to ninety, one hundred, or even longer. On the other hand, if you are feeling tired, bored and overly stressed most of the time, your "optimal longevity goal" may not extend much beyond dragging yourself out of bed the next morning!

By applying the principles presented in this book, you will experience the immediate health-related benefits you are seeking, while turning your life around and adding years—if not decades—to your projected life expectancy. If you are ready to accept this challenge—read on. Let's now move on to part two, which will take you on a detailed tour of the dimensions of wellness and provide you with specific "nuts and bolts" guidance on how to integrate a wellness lifestyle into your recovery program.

YOUR PRELIMINARY WELLNESS INVENTORY

1. **Life Goals:**
   - What goals in life are truly important to you? (Are you following your dreams, or have you lost touch with them?)
   - Do you believe that you will live to achieve these goals?
   - What is preventing you from pursuing these goals right now?

2. **Health Status:**
   - At present, how would you rate your overall state of health:
     a. Excellent
     b. Good
     c. Fair
     d. Lots of room for improvement

   - What *immediate health benefits* would you like to enjoy? (Check whatever applies—and add your own.)
     ❏ Increased energy and alertness
     ❏ Reduced stress
     ❏ Getting rid of the "tire" around my waistline
     ❏ Increased resistance to colds and flu

   Other immediate benefits you would like to enjoy:

   _____

3. **Longevity:**
   - How long would you ideally like to live, if you could count on reaching this age in a relatively good state of health?
   - Given your present state of health and your existing lifestyle, how long do you expect to live, if nothing remains unchanged?
   - What thoughts immediately come to mind in terms of steps that you might take to close the gap between the two figures?

Integrating the Cornerstones of Wellness into Your Recovery Program

In many respects, part two represents the heart of this book. In the pages ahead, we explore the various dimensions of wellness and discuss practical pointers for integrating each dimension into your daily life. Throughout this section we drive home the theme that by consciously adopting a wellness lifestyle, you place yourself in the driver's seat and reap the many benefits associated with high-level wellness. Let us begin our tour by taking an in-depth look at the critically important dimension of nutrition and recovery.

READER/CUSTOMER CARE SURVEY

We care about your opinions. Please take a moment to fill out this Reader Survey card and mail it back to us.
As a special **"thank you"** we'll send you exciting news about interesting books and a valuable **Gift Certificate.**

Please PRINT using ALL CAPS

First Name [   ] MI. [ ] Last Name [   ]

Address [   ]

City [   ] ST [ ] Zip [   ]

Phone # ([   ]) [   ] — [   ]   Fax # ([   ]) [   ] — [   ]

Email [   ]

(1) Gender:
___ Female   ___ Male

(2) Age:
___ 12 or under   ___ 40-59
___ 13-19   ___ 60+
___ 20-39

(3) Marital Status
___ Married
___ Single
___ Divorced/Widowed

(4) Did you receive this book as a gift?
___ Yes   ___ No

(5) How many Health Communications books have you bought or read?
___ 1   ___ 2-4   ___ 5+

(6) How did you find out about this book?
Please fill in ONE.
1) ___ Recommendation
2) ___ Store Display
3) ___ Bestseller List
4) ___ Online
5) ___ Advertisement
6) ___ Catalog/Mailing
7) ___ Interview/Review (TV, Radio, Print)

(7) Where do you usually buy books?
Please fill in your top TWO choices.
1) ___ Bookstore
2) ___ Religious Bookstore
3) ___ Online
4) ___ Book Club/Mail Order
5) ___ Price Club (Costco, Sam's Club, etc.)
6) ___ Retail Store (Target, Wal-Mart, etc.)

(9) What subjects do you enjoy reading about most? Rank only FIVE. Use 1 for your favorite, 2 for second favorite, etc.

	1	2	3	4	5
1) Parenting/Family	O	O	O	O	O
2) Relationships	O	O	O	O	O
3) Recovery/Addictions	O	O	O	O	O
4) Health/Nutrition	O	O	O	O	O
5) Christianity	O	O	O	O	O
6) Spirituality/Inspiration	O	O	O	O	O
7) Business Self-Help	O	O	O	O	O
8) Teen Issues	O	O	O	O	O
9) Sports	O	O	O	O	O

(14) What attracts you most to a book?
(Please rank 1-4 in order of preference.)

	1	2	3	4
1) Title	O	O	O	O
2) Cover Design	O	O	O	O
3) Author	O	O	O	O
4) Content	O	O	O	O

TAPE IN MIDDLE; DO NOT STAPLE

BUSINESS REPLY MAIL

FIRST-CLASS MAIL PERMIT NO 45 DEERFIELD BEACH, FL

POSTAGE WILL BE PAID BY ADDRESSEE

HEALTH COMMUNICATIONS, INC.
3201 SW 15TH STREET
DEERFIELD BEACH FL 33442-9875

FOLD HERE

Comments:

4

The Nutritional Hazards of Alcoholism and Drug Addiction

Sound nutrition is unquestionably a cornerstone of optimal health and lasting sobriety. Unfortunately, many—if not most—treatment programs fail to emphasize the pivotal role of nutrition.

The fact that our bodies replace each cell and tissue every seven years brings new meaning to the old saying "you are what you eat." In this chapter and the following one, we take an in-depth look at the relationship between diet, recovery and optimal health, in light of the critical association between nutritional

---

Note: The material presented in chapters 4 and 5 draws on concepts presented in the following publications. I am indebted to the authors for granting their permission to include these materials here:

Eating Right to Live Sober: A Comprehensive Guide to Alcoholism and Nutrition, Katherine Ketcham and L. Ann Mueller, M.D., Madrona Publishers, 1983.

Food For Recovery: The Complete Nutritional Companion for Recovering from Alcoholism, Drug Addiction, and Eating Disorders, Joseph D. Beasley, M.D. and Susan Knightly, Crown Trade Paperbacks, 1994.

Good Food for a Sober Life: A Diet and Nutrition Book for Recovering Alcoholics—and Those Who Love Them, by Jack Mumey and Anne S. Hatcher, Ed.D., R.D., Contemporary Books, Inc., 1987.

imbalances and substance abuse. We underscore the nutritional consequences of alcoholism and drug addiction, with particular reference to the alcohol-sugar connection. We also focus on the crucial importance of sound nutrition in safeguarding against relapse, paying special attention to nutritional considerations during early recovery. You will be given concrete recommendations for bringing your diet into balance, with special attention to the needs of people in recovery. You will also receive pointers for transitioning to an optimal diet that will become an integral part of your pathway to high-level wellness.

By way of background, let's take a quick look at where we stand as a society regarding our eating habits and their effect on our health.

The Link Between Diet and Optimal Health

The relationship between sound nutrition and optimal health is well established. For decades, leading health authorities have underscored the importance of a low-fat, high-fiber diet as a preventative measure against heart disease, the nation's number one killer. More recently, the American Cancer Society has gone on record as endorsing this same dietary regimen as an effective measure for reducing the risks associated with many cancers.

While the American public's level of knowledge concerning nutrition is at an all-time high, our ability to translate this knowledge into action leaves much to be desired. Most Americans rely on overly processed foods that are saturated with "empty calories" as their dietary mainstay, and we are suffering from a national epidemic of obesity. According to the Centers for Disease Control (CDC), over 30 percent of all adult Americans are now obese (defined as 30 percent or more above their ideal body weight), and close to two-thirds of all adults are either overweight or obese. Recent studies indicate that 15 percent of American children are either severely overweight or obese, and clinicians are now finding children as young as age three turning up with fatty deposits in their arteries. Not a pretty picture!

As a society, we are eating too much—especially high-fat, fast foods of questionable nutritional quality—and exercising far too little. Clearly, we need to devote some time to mastering the basics of optimal nutrition and incorporating them into our personal wellness programs. This is especially true for people in recovery.

As an alcoholic or addict, you were most likely chronically malnourished during your years of drinking and drugging. Consequently, you now have some major catch-up work ahead of you. Over the remainder of this chapter, we take a closer look at the nutritional consequences of alcoholism and drug addiction. Armed with this knowledge, you will then be ready to begin the process of transitioning yourself to a more optimal diet—a topic that we address in the following chapter.

The Nutritional Consequences of Alcoholism and Drug Addiction

Chances are, you have personally experienced the devastating effects of alcohol and other drugs on your body. While this discussion focuses primarily on the consequences of excessive alcohol consumption, the underlying concepts apply with equal force to virtually all addictive drugs, since their toxic effects universally conspire to throw our bodies out of balance.

Alcohol, the most widely abused drug, is a high calorie food with virtually no nutritional value. Habitual heavy drinking often results in chronic malnutrition because many drinkers unwittingly substitute the "empty calories" found in alcohol for the essential nutrients contained in healthy foods. An alcoholic who puts away a fifth of whiskey a day absorbs more than 2,200 calories from alcohol alone, leaving little room for tofu, veggies and other nutritious foods. Chronic heavy drinking also causes serious cumulative damage to various bodily systems, including the central nervous system, heart, liver and digestive organs. This cumulative damage results from the toxic effects of alcohol itself, together with the collective toll of malnutrition over years of excessive drinking.

Let's focus for a moment on alcohol's more insidious effects on our body and shed further light on why alcoholics are chronically undernourished.

- **Disruption of Appetite:** Alcohol has a disruptive effect on the brain's appetite control center, thus contributing to chronic malnutrition. Various stimulant drugs, particularly speed (methamphetamine) and cocaine, also depress the appetite control center, which is why these drugs are often abused as diet pills.

- **Alcohol Absorption and High-Fat Foods:** Alcohol is readily absorbed into the bloodstream directly from the stomach. Because high-fat food tends to slow alcohol absorption, bartenders throughout the world serve potato chips, beer nuts, and cheese and crackers along with their drinks, to enable their patrons to run up a healthy bar tab. This "high-fat braking" process explains why alcoholics develop a predisposition toward high-fat foods—often carrying this preference with them into their sobriety.

• **The Body's Processing of Alcohol as a Toxin:** The alcoholic's digestive system is constantly operating under damage control alert. Once alcohol enters the bloodstream, it goes almost immediately to the liver, which attempts to begin the process of detoxification. As alcohol has a poisonous effect on all organs, the body's highest priority is changing the toxic alcohol into nontoxic form; all other digestive functions are put on the back burner. Hence, when alcohol is present, vitamins and minerals (already in short supply in most alcoholics) are poorly absorbed and underutilized.

• **Disruption of Digestive Enzymes:** Alcohol disrupts the digestive enzymes that convert the foods we eat into substances needed by our bodies. Excessive alcohol consumption radically alters how the body digests proteins. Rather than effectively utilizing the proteins for their intended purposes, such as building blocks for muscles or brain cells, the amino acids that the proteins are composed of are converted into fat. So in place of firmly trimmed abdominal muscles, you are greeted by an ever-expanding "beer belly."

• **Alcohol's Unhealthy Diuretic Effect:** As every drinker is well aware, excessive alcohol consumption prompts us to beat a pathway to the rest room of our favorite bar, causing large amounts of water to be lost. Along with this loss of water, the body loses the water-soluble vitamins, such as vitamin C and the B vitamins, together with its supplies of various essential minerals that are also water soluble. Among other things, these minerals are important for muscle control and nerve transmission, in addition to building strong bones and teeth.

- **Hazardous Effects on Digestive System and Other Organs:** Over time, excessive alcohol consumption severely damages vital organs throughout the body, including the brain, liver, pancreas, kidneys, heart muscle and digestive system. Alcohol increases the buildup of stomach acid, which then attacks the lining of the stomach. Years of excessive alcohol consumption damages the walls of the stomach and intestines. This causes severe leakage of essential food substances before the body can effectively absorb and process foods for their intended purposes.

- **Disruption of Blood-Sugar Level:** One of the more damaging consequences of excessive alcohol consumption is the disruption of the body's blood-sugar balance, which can have particularly damaging effects on the central nervous system. As this action profoundly affects both sobriety maintenance and overall level of energy and alertness, we will take a closer look at this phenomenon.

The Alcohol-Sugar Connection

A growing number of physicians and nutritionists believe that most alcoholics suffer from alcohol-induced hypoglycemia—an abnormality of carbohydrate metabolism in which the mechanisms that regulate blood-sugar levels go wildly out of control.

Chemically, alcohol is a highly concentrated form of sugar. Excessive alcohol consumption causes erratic imbalances in blood-sugar levels. When you drink, your blood-sugar level rapidly rises and adrenaline is pumped to the brain. This "rush" is relatively short-lived, however, and blood-sugar levels proceed to drop below normal. The sudden rise and fall of blood-sugar levels observed in most alcoholics closely resembles the pattern classically associated with hypoglycemia, or chronic low blood sugar. If you're an active alcoholic, your body's blood-sugar regulating mechanisms are further thrown out of balance if you skip meals or eat food that is low in nutritional value.

Because alcohol raises blood-sugar levels temporarily, the drinker experiences an immediate "high" following the first drink. But soon, blood sugar drops below the baseline (normal) level. If you are an alcoholic, this "drop" prompts you to take another drink in an effort to recapture the initial high. Soon you are caught in an escalating cycle where your body is on a constant high/low blood-sugar "roller-coaster ride."

Unfortunately, this vicious cycle does not automatically end when you enter recovery. Indeed, many, if not most, recovering alcoholics/addicts carry into recovery the same erratic blood-sugar fluctuations that were previously associated with their heavy drinking. Why is this so?

When the alcoholic finally stops drinking, various organs and enzymes tend to be rather "slow on the uptake" in realizing that they must now function without the alcohol they have grown accustomed to. Previously, the alcohol had always been available as a "quick energy fix." During the initial months of sobriety, the body is literally in a state of physiological confusion and tends to fluctuate from one extreme to another. As Ketcham and Mueller report in *Eating Right to Live Sober,* many alcoholics in early recovery suffer from depression, irritability, mental confusion and disturbing mood swings. In many, if not most cases, the presence of these symptoms is largely attributable to wide blood-sugar fluctuations, together with depleted levels of B vitamins, calcium, magnesium and zinc—which adversely affect the central nervous system. These symptoms can be very frightening and may even trigger a relapse during the critical early months of sobriety.

In an effort to achieve both psychological and physiological equilibrium, alcoholics in early recovery are prone to heavy cravings for sweets as they strive to keep their blood sugar at the level that the body and brain require to function. In essence, the former addiction to alcohol is back-burnered and replaced by a newfound addiction to refined sugar. No doubt you've seen this pattern, and perhaps you have experienced it yourself. You consume gallons of coffee loaded with sugar, and ice cream, pastries, soda and candy become your dietary staples. While you never were a dessert person during your drinking days, you suddenly develop a ravenous craving for sweets. While before you would head out to your favorite tavern to tie one on after work, you now find yourself sneaking down to Baskin-Robbins for a double banana split. Or you visit your corner donut shop with a frequency that would put Homer Simpson to shame. Some trade-off!

The Negative Effects of Sugar and Other Nutritional Stressors

Without a doubt, we are a nation of sugar junkies. The average American consumes over 120 pounds of refined sugar each year—and the level consumed by many recovering alcoholics and addicts is even higher. Among other things, excessive sugar consumption increases the stress load on the body and causes the adrenal glands to overreact. Overtaxed adrenal glands leave us feeling chronically stressed out. A high sugar intake also depresses the immune system.

Excessive sugar consumption is clearly a contributing factor in heart disease, specifically because refined sugar is often consumed in foods such as ice cream and pastries, which are laden with saturated fats. In addition, when we overload the body with sugar, it automatically manufactures more cholesterol.

As if the detrimental effects of saturating our bodies with sugar weren't bad enough, the problem is further compounded by other nutritional stressors that make up the diets of many recovering people. Let's take a closer look at some of these other nutritional stressors.

Caffeine

At many, if not most, AA meetings, the seat next to the coffee urn is considered "the best seat in the house." While I don't want to rain on anyone's parade, we need to pause for a moment to consider the detrimental effects of excessive caffeine consumption. In addition to its ubiquitous presence in coffee, caffeine is found in concentrated form in most teas, cola beverages, chocolate and many over-the-counter medications.

Caffeine is an extremely powerful stimulant that serves to overstimulate the adrenal glands and elevate blood-sugar levels, causing a quick energy rush that is shortly followed by a "crash." Unfortunately, many recovering alcoholics/addicts radically increase their caffeine intake—drinking as many as fifteen, thirty or even fifty cups of coffee a day! In large doses, caffeine produces symptoms similar to amphetamine and cocaine intoxication, with an associated development of tolerance and physical dependency. Relapse prevention authority Terence Gorski observes that excessive caffeine consumption is clearly linked to diminished quality of sobriety and increased risk of relapse. This is especially true if you are recovering from addiction to cocaine or "speed," because heavy doses of caffeine can trigger cravings for your primary drug of choice.

Symptoms of caffeine overload include excessive anxiety and irritability, muscle spasms, insomnia and rapid breathing—together with irregular heart beat, increased blood pressure and higher cholesterol levels. Irritation of the lining of the stomach and intestines (which can lead to ulcers and gastritis) and damage to the kidneys and central nervous system are other effects. In addition, excessive caffeine consumption triggers mega-trips to the rest room, promoting loss of bodily fluids. This contributes to depletion of the body's supply of water-soluble vitamins and minerals. The detrimental effects of excess caffeine are compounded by the fact that most recovering alcoholics/addicts who are "caffeine junkies" are also sugar addicts, which adds insult to injury.

Am I suggesting that you give up coffee after already giving up alcohol and your other former drugs of choice? Not necessarily. However, if you currently drink more than two cups of coffee a day (or the equivalent caffeine dosage in the form of tea, sodas and chocolates), you should seriously consider either completely eliminating caffeine from your diet or cutting back to only two cups a day or less. For tips on how to do this, see the sidebar "Curbing Your Caffeine Consumption."

Curbing Your Caffeine Consumption

If you are overdosing on caffeine and wish to give it up (or cut back to two cups of coffee a day or less), the best time to do this is when you are feeling relatively free from pressing responsibilities. A quiet weekend is an ideal time to begin withdrawing from coffee.

Withdrawal Symptoms: Be prepared to experience withdrawal symptoms the first few days after discontinuing caffeine. These commonly include tiredness, irritability and headaches. Don't be surprised if you have occasional moments where you feel a bit "spacey" and even panicky. You can ease your withdrawal symptoms by taking walks, getting outdoors for some fresh air, listening to relaxing music and allowing yourself to get a bit of extra rest.

Hang in There: After a few days your body will begin to normalize and be able to "jump start" itself naturally, without the need for an artificial caffeine fix.

Tapering Off: If you have habitually been consuming five or more cups of coffee a day (or the equivalent amount of caffeine in the form of tea or cola beverages), you may want to reduce your caffeine intake gradually. Substitute green tea, other herbal teas or decaffeinated coffee—or drink spring water or fruit juice mixed with sparkling water instead of cola.

Helpful Substitutes: Green tea is an antioxidant that is relatively low in caffeine and is an excellent coffee substitute. You can also purchase decaffeinated green tea. Be sure to get the kind that has been naturally decaffeinated using spring water and effervescence, as this preserves the antioxidant properties in green tea. I enjoy starting my workday with a cup of decaffeinated green tea, and I look forward to a cup of licorice tea during my afternoon break.

Other Pointers: When I gave up caffeine over a decade ago, I found it very helpful to start my day with some "energizing imagery." The image that works best for me is to visualize the sun rising. I find this has a very energizing effect, and I've incorporated a few moments of "sunrise imagery" into my morning meditation for many years. I also find it very energizing to do a full set of morning exercises upon arising, and to treat myself to a wholesome breakfast after I have finished meditating.

Your 12-Step Support System: You may find it helpful to link up with a 12-stepper who has kicked the caffeine habit and who can act as an auxiliary sponsor while you are withdrawing from caffeine. You might also consider attending some Caffeine Anonymous meetings. Check with your local 12-step program's Central Office or contact directory assistance to see if there are any Caffeine Anonymous meetings in your area.

High-Fat and Highly Processed Foods

While you were drinking, you probably gravitated toward high-fat foods due to their "high-fat braking" effect on alcohol absorption. Chances are you have carried this preference for high-fat foods into your recovery.

As a nation, we are extremely reckless in our addiction to burgers, steaks, fries, ice cream, pastries and other high-fat foods. The typical American consumes a full 42 percent of their calories in the form of fats—including saturated fats, which account for 16 percent of total caloric intake. The pattern found in many recovering alcoholics and addicts is even worse, due to their addictive consumption of sweets and other high-fat foods.

Highly processed foods and high-fat foods are virtually the same when it comes to damaging the body. Fast foods, which now constitute the dietary mainstay of many Americans, tend to be very high in saturated fats—particularly the artery-clogging trans-fats found in french fries, taco shells and other foods fried in hydrogenated cooking oils. Gram for gram, fats are extremely high in calories while containing minimal amounts of vitamins, minerals and other essential nutrients. The high caloric concentration and low nutrient density that characterizes high-fat foods contributes to an overall feeling of low energy when we consume these foods in excess. Because nutrient-dense foods are necessary to repair the damage done by years of excessive drinking and drugging, people in recovery should limit their consumption of high-fat foods.

Food Additives

Highly processed foods, such as packaged foods, frozen and canned foods and most fast foods, tend to be laden with chemical substances added by the manufacturers to extend shelf life. Additives commonly found in processed foods include acidifying agents, bleaches, artificial dyes and flavorings, disinfectants and artificial sweeteners—the list goes on and on. These additives almost never add anything to the food's nutritional value, but they do place additional stress on the body. In addition, many food additives are potentially carcinogenic.

As a general rule, people whose systems are nutritionally and physiologically compromised—a grouping that includes virtually everyone in recovery from alcoholism and drug addiction—should take care to minimize their exposure to artificial food additives.

The Relapse Connection

As you can imagine, the collective toll of the "blood-sugar roller coaster" and other nutritional stressors that affect people in recovery often culminates in a chronic feeling of being "out of sorts." This problem can be particularly severe during the early months of recovery, when your body is undergoing a series of major readjustments. If left uncorrected, these nutrition-related symptoms can upset the delicate balance of recovery, tipping the scales in the direction of relapse.

The key to breaking this cycle is learning how to bring your diet into balance, while continuing to work your chosen recovery program diligently. In the following chapter, we will focus specifically on practical nutritional pointers for people in recovery.

CHAPTER

5

Your Nutritional
Foundation for Recovery

In chapter 4, I focused on the "bad news" of poor nutrition to underscore how critically important good nutrition is to anyone who is truly serious about their recovery. We reviewed the detrimental effects that cumulative malnutrition has on the body. We also focused on the tendency of many recovering alcoholics/addicts to succumb unwittingly to a variety of substitute food addictions—with particular reference to the hazards posed by excessive sugar consumption, overdosing on caffeine and overloading with high-fat foods.

Significantly, a growing number of authorities believe that the blood-sugar roller coaster triggered by addictive use of refined sugar and caffeine is a major contributing factor to relapse. While many people in recovery who persistently overdose on sugar, caffeine and other nutritional stressors manage to avoid the pitfalls of relapse, they often experience a less than optimal recovery as they constantly feel "wired" and suffer from chronic energy depletion. My goal is to help you experience the full joy of recovery and embrace the many good things that life has to offer.

If you have reason to believe that your nutritional status is less than optimal, don't despair. Now that we have gotten past all the gory details associated with poor nutrition, we can move on to the "good news." In this chapter I outline a variety of tools you can use to clean up your nutritional act. Most importantly, we will focus on how you can begin to *transition* toward a more optimal diet and *have fun* while you are making these changes. Read on!

Cleaning Up Your Nutritional Act

As a recovering alcoholic/addict, you need to pay particular attention to rebuilding your body via sound nutrition, adequate rest and vigorous physical exercise. You especially need to focus on developing eating habits that normalize your blood sugar throughout the day. You also need to learn to enjoy a diet that furnishes an abundant supply of nutrient-dense whole foods— foods that will provide your body with the essential nutrients it requires. The goods news is that once you master the nutritional basics, you will have a leg up on most Americans (whose diets are abysmally poor).

Mastering the Basics of Good Nutrition

A basic truism of life is that we must first learn to walk before we can run. So first, let's get the basics down—namely, three wholesome meals a day accompanied by sensible between-meal snacks. In line with most recovery-oriented nutritionists, I advocate eating three small meals, interspersed with three moderate snacks that provide good nutritional value. This pattern of eating helps normalize your blood sugar and promotes a positive energy level throughout the day.

In our fast-paced, production-oriented society, it's easy to get caught up in an unhealthy pattern of skipping meals and catching junk food on the run. You cannot afford to continue this pattern, however, if you are truly serious about your sobriety. To break this cycle, you need to consciously *take charge* and make sure that you get your basic "3 + 3" every day—that is, three small nutritious meals, accompanied by three nutritious snacks, spread out through the day.

Above all else, don't skip breakfast. When you skip breakfast, you start the day at a low energy level and are prone to overdosing on caffeine, sugar-laden snacks and other junk food. This is highly stressful to your body and impairs your ability to deal with day-to-day stresses effectively. In addition, skipping breakfast creates hunger pangs, which you may attempt to satisfy by overindulging in other meals and non-nutritious snacks. The predictable result is weight gain, accompanied by low energy levels throughout the day. Not a good combination!

Developing a Positive Addiction to Whole Foods

Whole foods, by definition, are foods that have been tampered with as little as possible. Ideally, your diet should include an abundant supply of organically grown fresh vegetables and fruits, together with whole grain breads and cereals. These foods should be grown in healthy soil that has not been overworked by excessive farming, and should be as free as possible from pesticides, antibiotics, dyes and other chemical additives. Seek out natural food stores and food cooperatives that specialize in organically produced foods. Don't be shy about asking their staffs any questions you may have concerning how the food was grown and processed before it arrived at their shelves.

While you may end up paying a bit more for organically grown whole foods than you would for their highly processed distant cousins that line supermarket shelves, remember the old saying: "Garbage in, garbage out."

Learning to "Add and Subtract"

If you are like most folks in recovery, you will benefit by eating a generous assortment of whole-grain foods, fresh vegetables, nuts, seeds and fresh fruit. At the same time, you should consciously focus on eliminating—or drastically cutting back on—all forms of junk food, including candy, sugary desserts, caffeine and refined foods. Later I'll give you some pointers for successfully negotiating these transitions.

Drinking Clean, Fresh Water

In addition to embracing whole foods as a dietary mainstay, you should be keenly aware of the importance of drinking clean, fresh water that is as free as possible from chemical contaminants. Because our bodies are composed mostly of water, clean, fresh water is one of the most essential nutrients. Unfortunately, it is also a much-endangered nutrient, as most public water supplies are heavily contaminated with pesticides (from agricultural runoff), chemicals and acid rain (from industrial pollution), and heavy metals (from old lead pipes and industrial pollution). As a recovering alcoholic/addict, you are already suffering from the toxic effects of your primary addictions. Your body's ability to detoxify the many chemicals found in public water supplies has most likely been seriously compromised.

Rather than relying on your local water purification plant for a healthy water supply (which would be a big mistake for most of us), resolve to treat yourself and your family to clean, fresh water either by drinking bottled spring water or installing a high-quality water filtration system. Sure, this may cost a few pennies a day, but it's a mere pittance compared to the tons of money that slipped through your fingers during your drinking and drugging days—right? After all, it's your body!

So there you have it: "Cleaning Up Your Nutrition Act 101." Now that we've gotten these basics under our belt, let's move on to "Nutrition 102," with a review of basic nutrients in terms of types of calories. Then we will focus our attention on guidelines for setting up a balanced diet, together with pointers for transitioning yourself toward an optimal diet for maintaining long-term sobriety and optimal health.

Bringing Your Diet into Better Balance: Nutrients by Calorie Type

The following is a brief review of basic nutrients by calorie type and the respective role each group plays in the nutritional scheme of things.

Carbohydrates

Carbohydrates are the primary source of calories (fuel) for the body's cells. They burn fast and easily to produce energy and heat. Carbohydrates are found almost exclusively in plant-derived foods—fruits, vegetables and grains.

There are two basic forms of carbohydrates—complex carbohydrates and sugars. Complex carbohydrates, also called starches, tend to be dense in essential nutrients when obtained from organically grown, unprocessed whole food sources. Complex carbohydrates are found in highly concentrated form in whole grain breads, cereal and pasta, potatoes, rice, corn and other vegetables, and fruits. Sugars are found in highly concentrated form in table sugar, syrups, honey and alcohol, and are also contained in fruits in the form of fructose.

As previously discussed, refined sugars and highly processed flours (as found in white breads) are essentially "empty calories" with little intrinsic nutritional value. Unfortunately, the diets of most people are laden with refined carbohydrates. At the same time, they are grossly deficient in the highly nutritious complex carbohydrates.

Proteins

Proteins are the essential "building blocks" for our bodies. The amino acids contained in proteins supply the raw materials from which our cells and tissues are composed. Protein-rich foods that contain all of the essential amino acids include fish, poultry and meat, soybeans, and dairy products. Various vegetable sources, in the form of grains and beans, also are important sources of protein. While individually these vegetable sources do not contain *all* of the essential amino acids you need, you can combine them in one meal to obtain the complete proteins that your body requires. Classic examples of complementary proteins include beans and rice, and pinto beans and corn bread.

As a recovering alcoholic/addict, it is critically important that your diet includes sufficient sources of protein. I encourage you to obtain most of your protein sources from the lighter end of the food chain, in order to minimize your intake of saturated fats. By the lighter end of the food chain, I am talking about beans, peas, other plant-based protein sources and other low-fat foods.

Fats

Carefully chosen dietary fats are essential to the body in moderate amounts. They are necessary for proper assimilation of the fat-soluble vitamins A, D, E and K. Most Americans, however, recklessly consume excessive quantities of fats, particularly in the form of saturated fats. This is particularly true for many recovering alcoholics who acquired a taste for fatty foods during their drinking days.

Dietary fats consist of saturated fats and unsaturated fats, which in turn break down into the monounsaturated and polyunsaturated fats.

Saturated fats are found primarily in animal products—particularly in red meats and dairy products—as well as in cocoa butter, palm oil and coconut products. You should attempt to minimize your consumption of saturated fats. They play a major role in the development of heart disease by contributing to the buildup of fatty deposits in coronary arteries.

Unsaturated fats, obtained from vegetable oils and fish oil, are the preferred source of dietary fat. Unfortunately, most commercially processed polyunsaturated oils—including safflower oil, corn oil, soybean oil, cottonseed oil, sesame oil, sunflower oil and margarine—have been overly processed and are linked with the production of free radicals within the body. Free radicals, which are also present in concentrated form in saturated fats, are highly destructive molecules that are major factors in the development of heart disease and many forms of cancer.

In summary, consume dietary fats in moderation. Pay particular attention to minimizing your intake of saturated fats and most commercially processed polyunsaturated fats. Generally speaking, your best sources of dietary fat are natural whole grains and seeds, various forms of fish, and unsaturated oils (e.g., extra virgin olive oil) that are as fresh and unprocessed as possible.

Specific Guidelines for a Balanced Diet

The following table, which summarizes recommended dietary breakdowns from the three caloric groups for people in recovery (with recommendations for food sources), is adapted from *Food for Recovery* by Joseph D. Beasley and Susan Knightly and is reproduced by permission of the authors.

Breakdown of a Balanced Diet for People in Recovery

Complex Carbohydrates	Proteins	Fats
65 percent	20 percent	15 percent or less;
(4 calories per gram)	*(4 calories per gram)*	only 1/2 saturated
		(9 calories per gram)

Vegetables and fruits	Grains/beans	Nuts
(fresh, preferably locally	*(complementary protein)*	Seeds
and/or organically grown)	Soy products	Oils *(cold-pressed)*
Grains and cereals *(whole*	Fish	Fish *(cold water)*
grain, minimally processed)	Poultry	Dairy foods*
Legumes *(e.g., beans, peas,*	Dairy foods*	Lean meats*
particularly in combination	Lean meats*	Some grains and
with grains)		beans
Grains/beans		
(complementary protein)		

*As these foods are high in both protein and fat, you need to consider both factors when making food choices.

A Closer Look at Dietary Guidelines for Recovery

Significantly, these dietary guidelines recommend that you obtain the majority of your calories (65 percent) from whole food sources rich in complex carbohydrates (as opposed to sugars). Whereas the average American derives a full 42 percent of his or her calories from fats (including 16 percent in the form of saturated fats), as a recovering alcoholic/addict, you should ideally reduce your fat consumption to only 15 percent of your daily caloric intake. You should also minimize your consumption of saturated fats by cutting back on red meat and dairy products.

This recommendation is very sound. It enables you to consume your calories efficiently and facilitate your body's rebuilding process by cutting back on fats. Instead, you are encouraged to eat highly nutritious complex carbohydrates and proteins, derived from whole food sources.

While the above guidelines recommend that you obtain 20 percent of your calories in the form of protein, other nutritional authorities recommend that protein should account for somewhere between 12 percent and 20 percent of your total calories. The important point is to make sure that you meet your daily protein requirements through a balanced diet centered around whole food sources—preferably favoring the lighter sources of protein depicted in the top rows of the table.

The Mediterranean Food Pyramid (Without the Wine)

I am sure that you are familiar with the Food Pyramid, published by the U.S. Department of Agriculture (USDA). While the USDA Food Pyramid provides some useful dietary pointers, I personally prefer the Mediterranean Diet Pyramid. The food allocations in that particular guide are more in line with nutritional requirements for most people in recovery. Presented below is an illustration of the Mediterranean Diet Pyramid, reproduced by courtesy of Oldways Preservation and Exchange Trust.

The Traditional Healthy Mediterranean Diet Pyramid

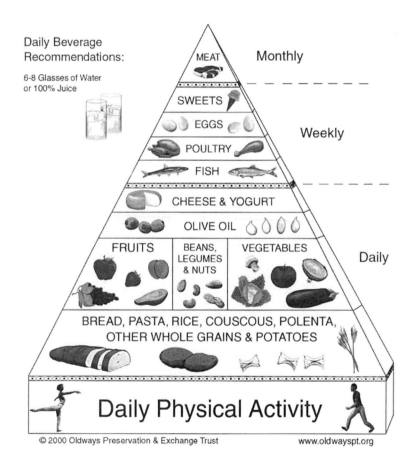

Daily Beverage Recommendations:

6-8 Glasses of Water or 100% Juice

Monthly

MEAT

Weekly

SWEETS

EGGS

POULTRY

FISH

Daily

CHEESE & YOGURT

OLIVE OIL

FRUITS

BEANS, LEGUMES & NUTS

VEGETABLES

BREAD, PASTA, RICE, COUSCOUS, POLENTA, OTHER WHOLE GRAINS & POTATOES

Daily Physical Activity

The Mediterranean Diet

Quite a bit has been written on the Mediterranean diet over the past decade, in view of the fact that residents of that region traditionally experience low rates of chronic disease and long life expectancies. This decidedly favorable health pattern appears to reflect the whole-foods based, semi-vegetarian diet enjoyed by many Mediterranean people. While red wine is also a dietary mainstay of this region, the wine has been eliminated from the following guidelines for obvious reasons.

The Mediterranean Diet Pyramid is a blended and balanced dietary approach, based on the proportions and frequency of servings for the various food groups—as suggested by their position on the pyramid.

The whole grain group, including whole grain breads and pasta, rice, cereals and potatoes, occupy a place of honor at the base of the pyramid. Include generous selections from this group with your meals throughout the day, together with liberal servings of fresh vegetables and fruits, shown in the next layer up. Beans and other legumes are also included in this layer, along with nuts. While highly nutritious, nuts should be consumed in moderation because they tend to be high in fat and calories. Soy protein, while not specifically shown in the pyramid, is an important member of the beans and legume group. Popular forms of soy protein include tofu and tempeh, which can be substituted for meat or chicken in many recipes to provide a delicious and highly nutritious plant-based whole protein source.

The third layer of the pyramid contains olive oil, a highly nutritious, monounsaturated fat that replaces other fats and oils as the principle source of dietary fat. You can use olive oil, together with rice vinegar, as a salad dressing and as a cooking oil in place of butter, margarine and other fats. Olive oil may also be used with whole grain bread or toast as a substitute for butter. Mix it with rice vinegar for a delicious bread "dip."

Also included in the pyramid layers recommended for daily consumption are dairy products in the form of cheese and yogurt. A variety of delicious low-fat cheeses are now available (along with nondairy soy cheeses), and nonfat yogurt makes a highly nutritious substitute for sour cream.

Moving into the layers of foods recommended for weekly consumption, we find fish, followed by poultry, eggs and sweets. Cold water fish, including salmon and halibut, are good sources of the omega-3 fatty acids, which have a beneficial effect in protecting our bodies against heart disease. My favorite "wellness guru," Dr. Andrew Weil, recommends several servings of cold water fish a week. (If you are a vegetarian, you can get your omega-3s from a variety of other sources, including soy protein and flaxseed oil.) Poultry and eggs may also be consumed in moderation as quality sources of protein. If poultry is part of your diet, try to purchase your chicken or turkey from a natural foods outlet that specializes in free-range poultry that have not been overloaded with hormones and antibiotics.

Significantly, foods containing refined sugar occupy a very small space near the top of the Mediterranean Diet Pyramid. From a recovery perspective this makes perfect sense, in view of the multiple hazards that sugar poses to people in recovery. Learn to back-burner your sweet tooth and instead include the many delicious forms of complex carbohydrates, including fresh fruits in season.

Finally, red meats, which contain high concentrations of saturated fats, appear at the apex of the pyramid, with the recommendation that they only be consumed a few times a month in modest quantities (if at all). In addition to their well known link with heart disease and their suspected contribution to many forms of cancer, many nutritionally oriented physicians also believe that red meats are implicated in the development of arthritis and other degenerative conditions. As an aside, I gave up red meats almost thirty years ago after watching the movie *Diet for a Small Planet,* and I have never missed them. This is especially true today, when there are so many delicious soy substitutes available in the form of veggie burgers and even veggie hot dogs!

Your New Diet:
Transitioning and Maintenance

Now that we have covered the basic components of a balanced diet for people in recovery, let's look at some specific suggestions to help you make the transition and stay with the program.

Start with Manageable Steps

A wellness lifestyle is a lifelong process of growth and development, and *you* set the pace. Commit yourself to undertaking manageable changes over time, and remember that small steps work better than giant leaps.

Your ability to effectively transition to a diet that is fully supportive of your long-term sobriety and pursuit of optimal health will hinge largely on your ability to organize your priorities and consistently follow through with your good intentions. Say, for example, that you would like to start transitioning toward a more nutritious breakfast. For the next two weeks, try replacing your usual "default breakfast" of black coffee laced with sugar (followed by those sugar donuts you grab on your way to work) with a nutritious breakfast built around oatmeal with banana and fresh fruit (and perhaps just a pinch of brown sugar), topped with low-fat milk. On days when you slip back into your "default" mode, observe how you feel in terms of decreased energy and alertness. Chances are, you will find that you feel better with a nutritious breakfast under your belt and will be motivated to experiment with other healthy breakfast options.

Essentially, I am recommending that you make a hobby out of your quest for optimal nutrition and enjoy the journey. Approach your dietary transitioning with a sense of adventure. Be prepared for many pleasant surprises as you begin to exercise your taste buds and gradually introduce more nutritious food options into your diet.

Get Off the Blood-Sugar Roller Coaster

By now, you are probably experiencing a love-hate relationship with your old friend, refined sugar. While you are developing an intellectual appreciation of the many hazards that sugar poses to people in recovery, you are probably not quite ready to rein in your sweet tooth. So let me try to guide you in renegotiating your relationship with sugary sweets in a way that will clearly give you the upper hand.

- Drastically cut back on your sugar intake by consciously substituting fresh fruit for desserts and substituting fruit juice in recipes calling for sugar.
- Have a *planned dessert* once, or at the most, twice a week. Plan desserts that are less disturbing to the biochemical balance of the body. For example, treat yourself to apple crisp or peach cobbler, as opposed to ice cream and rich pastries. Limit yourself to one reasonably sized serving and save your dessert until the end of a balanced, nutritious meal. And most important of all—be sure to *fully enjoy* your planned dessert without any feelings of guilt!

As previously discussed, in the interest of normalizing your blood-sugar levels it is also important to eliminate or minimize your consumption of caffeine. For example, form the habit of naturally energizing your body with vigorous aerobic exercise. (We treat this important topic more fully in chapter 6.)

Your Diet Transitioning "Cheat Sheets"

On the following pages you will find three "cheat sheets" designed to help you negotiate this important transitioning process. These include a set of guidelines entitled "A Sixty-Day Plan for Diet Transitioning," followed by a one-day sample menu planner utilizing the basic "3 + 3" guidelines discussed earlier, and finally, a daily diet log and menu planner.

Following the sixty-day plan should get you headed in the right direction. As a practicality, it is probably wise to plan on spending at least one year on fully integrating a wellness diet into your lifestyle—and your personal comfort zone. During this transitional period, continue following the basic guidelines in the sixty-day plan as you expand your comfort zone. While the following tools and guidelines are not intended to be a panacea, they are designed to help you lay a solid nutritional foundation for your recovery.

A SIXTY-DAY PLAN FOR DIET TRANSITIONING

The following pointers are designed to help you launch a successful diet transitioning process. Be innovative. Approach this project with a spirit of adventure and *have fun!*

Caution: If you are suffering from heart disease, diabetes or any other serious medical problem, be sure to consult your doctor concerning specific nutritional requirements dictated by your medical condition.

The First Thirty Days

Goal: To "get down the basics" and consciously start moving in the right direction.

Recommended Steps:
- Start each day with a wholesome, nutritious breakfast.
- Evaluate your eating patterns and begin substituting nutritious whole food choices for sweets and other "junk foods."
- Keep a daily log of your nutritional intake. This will help you catch yourself when you are "getting off the program."
- *Do not* skip meals. Consciously plan your daily menu to include three small nutritious meals interspersed with three nutritious snacks. If you're having difficulty doing this, seek out a good nutritionist who has experience working with people in recovery.

The Second Thirty Days

Goal: To continue integrating the basics of sound nutrition into your lifestyle, expanding your repertoire of creative, nutritious entrées and fine-tuning your nutritional behavior to conform with your individual needs and preferences.

Recommended Steps:

- Continue evaluating your eating habits with the goal of eliminating sweets and other junk foods in favor of a balanced and varied whole foods diet.
- Evaluate the role of caffeine in your life and take appropriate corrective action if indicated. (See sidebar on page 53, "Curbing Your Caffeine Consumption.")
- Buy a good nutrition book, begin reading it and add at least one new nutritious whole food entrée to your diet each week.
- Expand your repertoire of nutritious meals and snacks by sharing recipes with friends and coworkers and perhaps enrolling in a whole foods cooking class.
- Have fun with the process! Locate a good natural foods store where you can purchase organic whole food products, and roam the aisles seeking new ideas to incorporate into your menu planning. When dining out, look for restaurants that feature whole foods menus and ask your servers to help you choose nutritious entrées that will give your taste buds a well-deserved treat.

ONE-DAY SAMPLE MENU PLANNER

Note: The following examples are merely suggestions using the basic "3 + 3" formula of three small nutritious meals and three nutritious snacks. Get a good whole foods nutrition book and develop your own collection of *varied* selections.

Breakfast

- Oatmeal, with banana and other seasonal fresh fruit, topped with low-fat milk, rice milk or soy milk (and perhaps a small amount of brown sugar).
- *Or,* whole grain pancakes with unsweetened applesauce. One glass freshly squeezed orange juice.
- *Or,* nonfat yogurt, mixed in a blender with banana, other fresh fruit and museli.

Mid-Morning Snack

- Serving of fresh fruit (apple, banana, strawberry or whatever suits your fancy)
- *Or,* one slice whole grain toast, with either butter or unsweetened apple butter

Lunch

- ½ sandwich—turkey, tuna salad, soy cheese or tofu—served on whole-grain bread with reduced fat mayonnaise and lettuce, tomato and sprouts; small salad, or apple, banana or other fresh fruit.

Mid-Afternoon Snack

- Small serving trail mix (nuts, seeds and dried cranberries—unsweetened)
- *Or,* ½ whole grain bran muffin (unsweetened)
- *Or,* fresh fruit or raw vegetable sticks

Supper

- 2–4 ounces cooked salmon, brown rice mixed with wild rice; large salad featuring organic fresh vegetables, olive oil and rice vinegar dressing.
- *Or,* whole-grain pasta with marinara sauce mixed with sautéed mushrooms or "meatballs" made from lean ground turkey or soy protein; large salad (see above).
- *Or,* any other nutritious, delicious whole foods entrée, accompanied by a large salad or generous serving of broccoli or other cooked vegetables.

Late Evening Snack

- ½ cup museli grain cereal, with low-fat or rice milk
- *Or,* small serving trail mix (nuts, seeds, dried cranberries—unsweetened)

DAILY DIET LOG AND PLANNER

Use the left side of this form to plan your diet for the coming day, or use duplicate pages to plan an entire week. Then use the right side to record what you actually ate. This will help you monitor your progress.

Breakfast

_____   _____

_____   _____

_____   _____

Mid-Morning Snack

_____   _____

_____   _____

_____   _____

Lunch

_____   _____
_____   _____
_____   _____

Mid-Afternoon Snack

_____   _____
_____   _____
_____   _____

Supper

_____   _____
_____   _____
_____   _____

Late Evening Snack

_____   _____
_____   _____
_____   _____

Comments: How did I do today?

_____
_____
_____
_____
_____
_____

More on Successful Transitioning

Here are some additional pointers to help you successfully transition to a wellness diet that will fully support your goals of long-range sobriety and optimal health.

Read Up on Nutrition

Purchase a good, whole foods nutrition book, complete with recipes. Read this book sometime within the next sixty days and begin incorporating the recipes into your diet. The three books on nutrition and recovery cited at the beginning of chapter 4 all contain excellent whole foods recipes geared to people in recovery. If you are unable to obtain these books through your local bookstore, try ordering them through Amazon.com. Another excellent collection of whole foods recipes, emphasizing vegetarian entrées, is found in *Diet for a Small Planet,* by Frances Moore Lappé.

Choose Your Protein Sources Wisely

Unquestionably, protein should play an important role in the diet of anyone recovering from alcoholism or drug addiction. Proteins are the basic building blocks for our cellular tissue. Additionally, they play an important role in restoring the central nervous system's capacity to help keep our emotions in balance. While two to three daily servings of protein-dense foods are recommended, these foods do not need to dominate your meals. A two- to four-ounce serving of fish, poultry, soy or other foods rich in protein is sufficient. Develop the habit of obtaining your protein from the lower end of the food chain, particularly from the many delicious, nutritious entrees made with plant-based proteins. Purchase a vegetarian cookbook to learn about combining plant-based proteins to produce whole-protein meals.

Soy foods, most popularly available in the form of tofu and tempeh, are a highly nutritious, low-fat source of protein. My wife and I frequently dine on veggie burgers, and we use tofu and tempeh in stir-fries, tacos and even sandwiches. We also substitute soy cheeses for high-fat dairy cheeses, and I have found that soy ice cream makes a delicious substitute for dairy ice cream.

Strive to Maintain Your Proper Weight

Maintain your weight through an optimal balance of exercise and sound nutrition. Every sixth grader knows that the only sure way to lose weight is to burn more calories through exercise than what you take in as food. Yet how many of us really put this into practice?

As you make a conscientious effort to build your diet around nutritious foods and start the exercise program outlined in the following chapter, your body weight will begin to normalize. If you want to lose weight, pursue a realistic weight-loss goal of one to one and a half pounds a week through a combination of exercise and sensibly cutting back on calories. As in all aspects of wellness, motivation and persistence is the key.

Incidentally, if you are constantly losing weight by dieting, only to put the pounds right back on within the next few months, you might want to ask yourself *why* you are overeating. Perhaps you are trying subconsciously to compensate for something that may be lacking in your life at a deeper level, in the realm of relationships and personal fulfillment. We address that topic more fully in chapter 9, which takes an in-depth look at personal fulfillment and the spiritual dimension of wellness.

Guard Against Nutritional Hazards in Your Workplace

Many modern-day workplaces are minefields strewn with nutritional hazards: leftover desserts brought in by coworkers, donuts and pastries proffered by well-intentioned managers, candy bars hidden in desk drawers and vending machines stocked with "empty calorie" selections. In our fast-paced society, workaholism and junk food addiction go hand in hand. The key to sidestepping workplace food hazards lies in planning ahead. Unless your company features a cafeteria offering a well-stocked salad bar and other nutritious foods, bring in a healthy lunch and your own nutritious snacks. And "just say no" to all the questionable goodies floating around the office!

Seek Out Appropriate Treatment for Eating Disorders

Many people in recovery, particularly women, suffer from eating disorders. The most prevalent eating disorders are anorexia nervosa and bulimia. People suffering from anorexia tend to be perfectionists. They become overly obsessed with maintaining a trim figure and literally end up starving themselves. At the opposite end of the spectrum is bulimia, or "binge and purge" eating, in which a person habitually "pigs out" on junk foods, such as ice cream, pastries and pizza, and then induces vomiting in the hope of avoiding weight gain. Eating disorders among people in recovery are often substitute addictions, in which the person's compulsive/addictive behaviors are transferred from alcohol and drugs to food. Eating disorders are serious and require medical attention. They are also highly treatable. If you suspect you may be suffering from an eating disorder, be sure to discuss this with your doctor and obtain appropriate treatment.

The Role of Nutritional Supplements

When combined with a balanced, whole foods–based diet, vitamin and mineral supplements can help our bodies repair damaged cells and tissues, mitigate stress and illness, strengthen our immune systems, promote increased energy and alertness, and help protect the body's cells from pollutants in the air we breathe, the food we eat and the water we drink. As a recovering alcoholic/addict, you have an additional incentive to consider taking daily vitamin and mineral supplements—the devastating effects of alcohol and drugs on your body's ability to effectively absorb and use essential nutrients.

Nutritional supplements are not "magic bullets," however, and no one should rely on them as a substitute for a well-balanced, whole foods diet. In other words, you cannot gorge yourself with fast foods and then try to play nutritional catch-up by megadosing on vitamin, mineral and herb concoctions. You also need to be aware that excessive doses of vitamins and minerals are wasted by the body and can even alter the chemistry of your body and promote an artificial dependency on them. Finally, keep in mind that excessive doses of certain vitamins—particularly vitamins A,

D and E—can cause damage to the liver and other organs.

The following chart offers guidelines to recovering alcoholics and addicts for daily nutritional supplementation. It is designed to promote overall health and well-being, as well as long-term recovery. The chart is adapted from recommendations made by Katherine Ketcham in *Beyond the Influence* (Bantam Books, 2000) and is presented with the author's permission. While the dosages presented are generally considered safe and nontoxic, it is always wise to seek the advice of your physician or another trained health professional before taking these or other nutritional supplements.

RECOMMENDED NUTRITIONAL SUPPLEMENTATION FOR RECOVERING ALCOHOLICS AND ADDICTS*

Basic Daily Formula: A standard multivitamin pill providing approximately 100 percent of the recommended daily allowance (RDA) for most vitamins, minerals and trace elements.

Additional Recommended Supplementation:

Vitamin A (beta-carotene or mixed-carotene)
- Purpose: an antioxidant that helps support the immune system and prevent night blindness
- Dosage: 10,000 to 25,000 IU daily

B-Vitamin Complex
- Purpose: aids physiological and neurological processes that help us cope with stress; improves nervous system functioning; helps maintain health of vital organs
- Dosage: B-100 complex daily

Vitamin C

- Purpose: stimulates immune system; an antioxidant that helps maintain healthy blood vessels
- Dosage: 1,000 to 3,000 milligrams daily (divided into two to three smaller doses throughout the day)

Vitamin E

- Purpose: an antioxidant that improves functioning of heart and muscle cells and reduces cardiovascular risk
- Dosage: 400 to 800 IU daily (Note: always take d-alpha tocopherol—natural vitamin E—which is the most active form of the vitamin)

Omega-3 Fatty Acids

- Purpose: anti-inflammatory agents that promote good cardiovascular health; also promote increased production of serotonin, which helps combat depression. Omega-3 fatty acids are polyunsaturated fatty acids. Two types of omega-3s—eicosapentaenoic acid (EPA) and docosahexaenoic acid (DHA)—are found in fish and fish oils. A third type, gamma-linolenic acid (GLA), is found in some vegetable oils and dark green leafy vegetables, and in some fruits and nuts.
- Dosage:
  Eat two to three servings weekly of omega-3–rich fish, such as salmon, mackerel, anchovies and albacore tuna
  Or, take a 1,500-milligram omega-3 supplement daily
  Or, take 1,500 milligrams evening primrose oil daily
  Or, take a daily GLA supplement in the form of black currant seed oil or borage seed oil

*Source: *Beyond the Influence,* by Katherine Ketcham and William F. Asbury, Bantam Books, 2000.

These guidelines present a reasonably balanced approach to vitamin and mineral supplementation designed to address the basic needs of many people in recovery. If you choose to supplement with vitamin A, mixed carotenes are generally recommended as the preferred source. Be careful not to overdose with vitamin A, as excessive doses can have a toxic effect. If you are suffering from liver damage, be sure to consult your physician before taking any form of vitamin A.

The role of the B vitamins in strengthening our resiliency in coping with day-to-day stresses is well documented, and moderate supplementation with B vitamins probably makes sense for most people.

In recent years there has been a bit of controversy surrounding appropriate dosages for vitamin C supplementation, and this is one area where I tend to depart from the recommendations presented in the preceding chart. While some experts claim that vitamin C can help detoxify the liver and lessen acute alcohol withdrawal symptoms, other authorities caution that habitually taking large doses of vitamin C can foster an artificial dependency on megadoses. Nutrition expert Dr. Andrew Weil currently recommends meeting our daily vitamin C requirements through a diet rich in fresh fruits and vegetables, and perhaps taking a modest supplemental dosage of 200 milligrams daily as "insurance." (My own supplementation with vitamin C currently falls in line with Dr. Weil's recommendations.)

In reference to vitamin E, health and nutrition authorities generally recommend daily maintenance dosages ranging between 200 and 800 IU per day in order to obtain the maximum antioxidant benefits for safeguarding against heart disease.

Omega-3 fatty acids are important to people in early recovery because these nutrients help combat depression through promoting increased serotonin production. (Serotonin increases feelings of well-being.) They also aid in the brain's production of neurotransmitters. This is important as the neurotransmitters help keep your emotions in balance.

Again, your wisest course of action regarding nutritional supplementation is to consult a physician or a nutritionist—preferably someone with special expertise in nutrition and recovery —concerning your individual requirements. Alternatively, I would recommend visiting a reputable health food store to locate a combination formulation that essentially falls in line with the recommendations presented in the chart; add individual supplements to this basic formula as appropriate.

Another alternative is using the services of one of the companies that produce vitamin and mineral formulas to address the special needs of people in recovery. Two firms that I am familiar with are:

Addiction End Institute. This company distributes the Natural High Neurotransmitter Restoration Formula, a compound formulated by Joseph D. Beasley, M.D., co-author of *Food For Recovery*. For further information, visit their Web site at *www.addictionend.com.*

Pacific Biologic. This company is based in Clayton, California. Contact them at 1-800-869-8783.

In addition to these general recommendations some specialists in nutrition and recovery recommend supplementation with L-glutamine, a protein derivative that purportedly helps curb cravings for alcohol, drugs and sugar. Supplementation with milk thistle may also be beneficial in some cases, as there is some evidence suggesting that milk thistle can assist a damaged liver in rebuilding and repairing itself. Consult a physician or other reliable health professional for advice concerning appropriate dosages.

Important: Do *not* attempt to self-medicate with these or any other supplements, over and beyond the recommended basics. Again, many nutritional supplements have dependency-producing properties and can be toxic when consumed in large doses. Your wisest course of action, by far, is to consult a physician who is knowledgeable in the area of a nutrition and recovery regarding your specific requirements for supplementation.

Obtaining Help from the Experts

In this chapter you have learned about a variety of tools that can assist you in getting your nutritional act together. Following through with these recommendations should give you a solid nutritional foundation for recovery. You may also want to consider consulting either a physician or a nutritionist with special expertise in working with recovering alcoholics and addicts. These experts can assist you in fine-tuning a nutritional program. In particular, I highly recommend seeking out expert assistance in situations where any of the following conditions are present:

- You have a history of medical problems, such as liver damage, diabetes or heart disease, which require ongoing medical supervision.
- You discover that you are encountering serious difficulties in applying the various recommendations for dietary transitions presented in this chapter; you also find that you keep

returning to self-destructive eating patterns that threaten to undermine your sobriety.

- You are currently suffering from anorexia, bulimia or another eating disorder.
- You have a history of repeated relapse to alcohol and/or drugs and have never been able to free yourself successfully from the "blood-sugar roller coaster."

Where should you go to seek out competent help in dealing with these types of problems?

If you have recently relapsed, you might want to seek out a treatment program that employs a nutritionally oriented approach to facilitating recovery. Such a program should include individualized nutritional evaluation and counseling services provided by dieticians or nutritionists with special expertise in this area. Do some research to locate treatment programs in your area that incorporate a nutritionally oriented approach. Question their staffs concerning what dietary guidelines they employ in primary treatment, and how nutrition and recovery are addressed in their continuing care program.

For assistance in finding a physician with special expertise in addictive disorders, contact your local medical society to see if they can initiate a referral, or contact the American Society of Addiction Medicine in Chevy Chase, Maryland, at 310-656-3920.

Resources that may be able to assist you in locating a competent, recovery-focused nutritionist include treatment centers, a physician who specializes in addiction medicine, your local 12-step program's Central Office (as well as your fellow 12-steppers) and the dietary department of your health plan or a local hospital. When contacting your health plan or a hospital, be sure to specify that you are seeking a dietician with special expertise in working with recovering alcoholics and addicts. This is important, as not all dieticians have special training in this area.

In summary, I hope you will enthusiastically embrace your nutritional foundation for recovery as you pursue your path to wellness. Again, do not try to make drastic changes overnight. Rather, your goal should be to take small steps in *transitioning* toward a diet that will serve you well for the rest of your life. As you have a long time ahead of you, take it easy and *enjoy the journey!* Now, let's shift gears and look at an equally important dimension of wellness and recovery—engaging in active physical exercise to build a strong foundation for lasting sobriety and optimal health.

6

Physical Exercise:
Fitness and Recovery

P hysical exercise is unequivocally one of the most important components of the pathway to optimal health. Engaging in vigorous exercise on a regular basis represents one of the best forms of "health insurance" you can give yourself.

This chapter discusses the importance of physical exercise to successful sobriety maintenance and to enhancing your overall state of health. If you are currently engaged in a regular exercise program, this chapter will reinforce what you are already doing and help you fine-tune those efforts. If you are not exercising on a regular basis, you will learn why you need to exercise as a person in recovery. You also will receive step-by-step guidance about how to custom-tailor an exercise program to your needs and lifestyle preferences.

Benefits Associated with Exercise

The benefits associated with exercise are legion. People who exercise regularly enjoy increased alertness and vitality, improved self-esteem, and greater resistance to disease. Regular exercisers are more readily able to maintain their proper weight, enjoy improved muscular strength and flexibility, and experience significant psychological benefits. These include an increased sense of well-being, improved ability to manage stress, relief from mild depression and improved self-confidence in social relations. Documented improvements in alertness and performance associated with exercise have prompted leading *Fortune 500* companies to sponsor corporate fitness centers for their employees. As we will also show, regular exercise offers important safeguards against relapse.

Aerobic exercise improves the efficiency of our heart and lungs and is positively associated with reduced risk of heart disease. Compared to nonexercisers, people who regularly engage in aerobic exercise have approximately half the risk of developing heart disease and an even lower risk of sudden death associated with a heart attack. Regular exercise also appears to be associated with reduced risk of many forms of cancer. In fact, recent research suggests that exercise can even substantially improve women's chances of surviving breast cancer. As a group, exercisers enjoy significantly longer life spans and frequently enjoy a high level of health and physical vigor into their eighties, nineties and beyond.

Regular exercise can even help strengthen your immune system and contribute to increased resistance to the common cold. In a study recently reported by the American College of Sports Medicine, which focused on a group of 547 healthy adults, study participants who regularly engaged in brisk walking and other forms of moderate intensity exercise reported 20 percent fewer colds over the course of a year than subjects who did not exercise. As we will demonstrate throughout this book, wellness is a synergistic process. People who exercise regularly are much more likely to also follow healthy diets and avoid cigarette smoking and other unhealthy behaviors.

One of the most powerful immediate benefits associated with exercise lies in the realm of stress reduction. I know from personal experience that when I go for a day or two without exercising, my stress level shoots up and I start climbing the walls! As we will elaborate in chapter 7, our fast-paced, modern lives constantly bombard us with a variety of stresses that do not lend themselves to immediate resolution. Typically, we tend to lock these stresses into our bodies. This can take a variety of forms, including chronic tension in our backs, necks and shoulders, elevated blood pressure and other physical manifestations. Vigorous exercise provides a natural and effective way of releasing these stresses from our bodies, pumping rich oxygen through our bloodstream, and enabling our muscles and other bodily systems to return to their normal, relaxed state.

Let's now focus on the specific benefits of exercise in helping prevent relapse and maintain sobriety.

Benefits Associated with
Recovery and Relapse Prevention

Regular physical exercise is an important part of any sound program for preventing relapse and promoting long-term sobriety. Running, brisk walking and other forms of vigorous exercise serve as effective substitutes for alcohol and drugs, while at the same time contributing to marked improvements in self-esteem, vitality and alertness. If you are in the early stages of recovery, engaging in regular exercise will help take the edge off the various stresses associated with early sobriety. If you are an "old-timer," exercise can play an important role in helping you experience the full joy of sobriety.

Significantly, vigorous exercise contributes to the production of endorphins, chemical messengers that trigger the pleasure centers in the brain. The so-called "runner's high" is largely attributable to the impact of endorphins released into our systems when we exercise. Recent research suggests that addictive use of various drugs, particularly opiates and stimulants, may interfere with the body's natural ability to produce endorphins and release them into the bloodstream. It stands to reason, therefore, that the increased production of endorphins that accompanies vigorous exercise may help ward off relapse by reducing cravings for one's former drugs of choice.

A growing body of evidence attests to the benefits of exercise associated with relapse prevention and sobriety maintenance. In a classic Canadian study, which focused on alcoholics completing residential treatment, David Sinyor and his associates found that a full 69 percent of subjects who engaged in vigorous exercise as part of their treatment were able to successfully maintain sobriety following treatment. In contrast, 62 percent of subjects who completed treatment without the exercise component relapsed to drinking within three months following treatment. Another study, employing a battery of psychological tests, found that alcoholics completing a residential treatment program that included a structured exercise program fared significantly better in terms of anxiety and depression than did subjects who completed treatment without the exercise component.

My own research, focusing on alcoholics/addicts who successfully stayed clean and sober following treatment, versus those who relapsed, demonstrated a positive association between involvement in vigorous exercise and reduced likelihood of relapse. In my study, subjects were asked to assign themselves to one of the following categories:

- **Heavy Exercisers:** subjects who reportedly engaged in vigorous exercise (such as running or jogging) for twenty minutes or longer, *at least* three times a week.
- **Moderate Exercisers:** subjects who engaged in vigorous exercise one or two times a week.
- **Light Exercisers:** subjects who rarely engaged in vigorous exercise.

Significantly, a full 52 percent of subjects in the successful recovery group fell into either the heavy or moderate exercise categories, compared with only 28 percent of the subjects who relapsed following treatment. Taken together, these studies underscore the powerful benefits associated with regular exercise in helping you stay clean and sober.

Let's turn to the practical applications of exercise to wellness and recovery. First, we will highlight the three essential types of exercise recommended and the major benefits associated with each. Second, we will provide you with step-by-step guidance on how to launch a personalized exercise program.

Your Personal Exercise Program

Ideally, your personal wellness program should include regular participation in each of the following basic forms of exercise:

1. **Aerobic exercise**—exercise which challenges your heart and lungs to a level approaching maximum capacity. Popular forms of aerobic exercise include jogging, aerobic dance, swimming laps, bicycling and tennis. Brisk walking is another excellent form of aerobic exercise, if you walk long enough to gain the full aerobic benefits.

2. **Flexibility exercise**—exercise which stretches your various limbs and joints to promote increased flexibility. It is important to engage in stretching exercises for several minutes before and after a vigorous aerobic workout, in addition to performing a daily set of stretching exercises to promote maximum flexibility. Popular forms of flexibility exercises include yoga and tai chi, as well as general flexibility exercises recommended by physical fitness instructors and trainers. (Yoga, tai chi and other forms of moving meditation also offer important calming and centering benefits.)

3. **Muscle toning or resistance-training exercise**—exercise designed to strengthen your various muscular systems. Popular forms of resistance training include weight lifting and working out with a rowing machine or other exercise equipment.

Getting Started: Practical Guidelines

If it has been a while since you exercised on a regular basis, all these exercises may appear a bit intimidating. Don't despair. As with every aspect of wellness and recovery, we will break it down into manageable components that you can tackle one step at a time.

Following are some basic pointers to help you get started.

Assess Your Level of Fitness and Obtain Medical Clearance

Your current level of fitness is determined by such factors as your age, your present level of physical activity, and the presence or absence of any health conditions that may require you to modify your exercise program.

Many community colleges offer adult conditioning programs, which include an expert evaluation of a participant's "going in" level of fitness and the development of a personalized "exercise prescription." Many health clubs provide a similar service.

If you haven't engaged in regular exercise for some time, you should discuss your plans with your primary physician. This is particularly true if you are over forty or have a personal history of heart disease, hypertension, diabetes, arthritis, obesity or any other health conditions that may affect your ability to engage in regular, vigorous exercise. Most physicians are attuned to the many benefits of exercise and will support your desire to launch an exercise program. Similarly, your doctor can offer sound counsel concerning any precautions you should take in developing an exercise program.

Choose Fun Exercises That Fit Your Current Lifestyle

It's critically important to choose a type of exercise that you enjoy—or believe that you can learn to enjoy—otherwise you won't stay with it. Equally important, choose exercise that is a realistic fit with your current lifestyle and ongoing responsibilities.

Using myself as an example, I currently have an exciting yet stressful full-time job that entails a two-hour round-trip commute daily. I am working on this book in my spare time, and I place a premium on enjoying quality time at home with my wife. Given the constraints associated with my current lifestyle, a daily lunchtime program of brisk walking for forty-five minutes fits in perfectly with my schedule.

Get Expert Guidance

As discussed in the next section, the federal Centers for Disease Control and the American College of Sports Medicine (CDC/ACSM), along with the Institute of Medicine, have issued exercise guidelines. They collectively urge adult Americans to strive for between thirty and sixty minutes of moderate-intensity physical activity each day. The experts believe this level of daily exercise promotes cardiovascular fitness and general health benefits. The good news is that you can start small and gradually increase your daily activity threshold. You can also meet your quota through a series of "mini exercise breaks," lasting ten to fifteen minutes or longer.

Dr. Andrew Weil, director of the University of Arizona's Program in Integrative Medicine, recommends a program of brisk walking, forty-five minutes per session, five days a week. Walking is an excellent form of exercise for promoting overall fitness, and it is a convenient exercise that almost everyone can engage in. Weil advises walkers to wear supportive shoes with well-cushioned heels, to practice good posture while walking and to start out slow, gradually building up to a goal of walking thirty to forty-five minutes at least five days a week. It's also a good idea to vary your walking route and to walk in pleasant surroundings whenever possible.

Dr. Weil also recommends doing some form of muscle-building or resistance-training exercise, ideally at least two or three times a week. Resistance training is particularly important in warding off the muscle atrophy associated with aging. Popular forms of resistance training include weight lifting, push-ups, and working out with rowing machines and other forms of exercise equipment. You can work some resistance training into your daily walk by holding a two- to three-pound weight in each hand and swinging your arms while walking.

One word of caution regarding resistance training—get expert guidance before getting started. You want to avoid damaging your muscles or limbs by overdoing it, and you should receive expert instruction in working at a pace and level of intensity that is in line with your level of fitness and overall fitness goals. Again, many community colleges and health clubs offer programs that can assist you in this area.

Join a Health Club/Exercise Group or Find an Exercise Buddy

Many people enjoy the social benefits of working out in a group setting. If you are just getting started, the social support provided by a group or exercise buddy might be just what you need to "hang in there" until exercise becomes second nature. Consider joining a hiking or biking club, linking up with a health club, or taking an exercise class. Many treatment centers sponsor alumni associations that offer a variety of activities. Check out whether your alumni association offers a walking club or other form of structured exercise program. If they don't, volunteer to start one!

Start Small and Build Up Gradually to Your Goal

Phase yourself in over several months. For example, if brisk walking is your chosen form of exercise, start with walking ten to fifteen minutes every day. When you feel comfortable with that routine, start adding five minutes to your daily walk until you reach your goal of walking thirty to forty-five minutes, five days a week.

Recommended Physical Activity for Adults

CDC/ACSM Exercise Guidelines

In 1995, the CDC/ACSM together issued the following recommendation concerning the level of physical activity needed to produce significant health benefits:

Every U.S. adult should accumulate thirty minutes or more of moderate-intensity physical activity on most, preferably all, days of the week.

The current CDC/ACSM guidelines portray a practical goal that people with busy lifestyles can embrace. The guidelines also take into account the mounting evidence that daily physical activity at this level is associated with substantial health-related benefits. The CDC/ACSM guidelines emphasize:

- The significant health benefits associated with moderate-intensity physical activity (for example, walking briskly at three to four miles per hour, cycling for pleasure, playing table tennis and doing many household chores).
- The growing evidence that suggests we can accumulate our daily threshold of physical activity in relatively short multiple bouts, lasting ten to fifteen minutes per "mini-session."

Institute of Medicine Guidelines: Raising the Bar

In 2002, the Institute of Medicine "raised the bar" on exercise guidelines by issuing a report recommending an hour of moderate-intensity exercises each day, for purposes of promoting good health and maintaining optimal body weight. The Institute of Medicine recommendation is based on studies of people with healthy body weights and were designed to measure how much energy (in the form of calories) these people take in and use up in a given day.

Where Do You Stand?

Whether you choose to follow the CDC/ACSM recommendation or the more rigorous Institute of Medicine guidelines, just keep in mind that a daily exercise regimen based on moderate-intensity physical activity is well within the reach of virtually everybody. And you can achieve your daily activity threshold through a series of relatively short bouts. I personally advocate building up to a daily concentrated block of moderate-intensity activity (such as brisk walking or bicycling) of thirty minutes or longer. Supplement this core exercise block with "mini-bouts" of exercise you can do throughout the day. This puts a positive spin on those household chores and yard work that you have been putting off, as these activities also count toward meeting your daily quota. The important thing is to get moving—and be persistent!

Additional Exercise Pointers

The following pointers will help you fully integrate your exercise program into your lifestyle, while deriving maximum benefit and enjoyment from the process.

Make Exercise Fun—Visualize the Desired Results

Rather than being a chore, exercise should be an enjoyable part of your daily life. Experiment with different forms of exercise until you find one you enjoy, then stick with it. Whenever possible, exercise in a pleasant setting that enhances your overall feeling of serenity and well-being.

When you are just beginning your exercise program, it is particularly important to visualize the results you want to attain. Just before drifting off to sleep at night, or in the morning upon awakening, take a few minutes to close your eyes and see yourself working your exercise program. Visualize yourself becoming stronger and more resilient, and enjoying newfound levels of vigor, vitality and alertness. You might also choose to visualize yourself participating in new and exciting activities because of your increased state of fitness—such as climbing a mountain or running a marathon.

While I am encouraging you to start small and continue to raise the bar, it's even more important to enjoy the process. In exercise, as in all aspects of wellness, beyond a wholesome discipline, be gentle with yourself.

Build Exercise into Your Schedule— Then Stick with It!

If you are like most readers, you are dealing with an overly crowded schedule and constantly juggling a million different things.

Nevertheless, I strongly urge you to make exercise a *priority* and stick with your program. Make exercise appointments with yourself, reschedule them if necessary and identify any obstacles that you are encountering. When I first started exercising, I would plan a series of noontime workouts throughout the week, which often ended up being sabotaged due to pressing business priorities. I soon learned that I needed to be willing to reschedule my "exercise appointments" to the evening on those days when I got snagged into unexpected noontime business commitments.

In launching your exercise program, it is very important to tune in to your natural rhythm and identify the times of day and days of the week that work best for you. If you are an early riser, you may feel naturally inclined to start your day off with a vigorous workout. Or, if you are like me, you may welcome a noontime session as a welcome break from the day's routine.

Spread your exercise program out throughout the week and

avoid becoming a "weekend warrior." If you go all week without exercising and try to "make it up" on the weekend, you are setting yourself up for strains, sprains and other injuries that happen when our bodies are out of condition.

Build Flexibility Exercises into Your Daily Routine

We all need to engage in daily flexibility exercises as a preventative measure against arthritis, back trouble, and muscle and joint stiffness. If you already suffer from any one of these conditions, it is critically important that you practice appropriate therapeutic exercises on a daily basis.

The best time for flexibility exercise is early in the morning, right after your morning shower. Take five to ten minutes or longer to go through a series of gentle stretches. If your doctor or physical therapist has prescribed therapeutic exercises for you, be sure to include these in your morning routine. An added benefit of daily stretching exercises is that a flexible body makes for a more flexible mind.

Supplement Regular Exercise with "Exercise Perks"

Add variety to your program. Exercise in different locations and experiment with different forms of exercise. On weekends, supplement your regular exercise program by hiking, biking, mountain climbing or whatever else appeals to you. Plan a vacation where you can hit the trails and clear your head. Living in Southern California, which represents the epitome of living in the fast lane, I take a weekend hike in the desert every chance I get. I also look forward to our annual vacation in the High

Sierras, where we climb the peaks and treat our lungs to the clear mountain air. Over the years, I have found hiking in nature to be extremely healing in terms of experiencing true serenity and reconnecting with the spiritual side of life.

If you have a sedentary job, be sure to take several "mini-exercise breaks" throughout the day. Several times a day, I take a break from my desk to walk through the building and clear my head. I return to my desk refreshed and invigorated. I often find that the solution to a problem I've been wrestling with spontaneously "pops up" in the middle of one of these mid-day walks. If you do a lot of work with a computer, it is very important to take brief computer breaks throughout the day where you stand and stretch, and break the cycle of muscular tension associated with intense computer work. Other good ways of incorporating exercise into your workday include climbing the stairs instead of taking the elevator and parking several minutes away from your workplace to give yourself a bit of extra walking.

Remember: Don't Overdo It

Relapse prevention authority Terence Gorski notes that while many recovering people get little or no exercise—to the detriment of their physical health—others go to the opposite extreme and become overly obsessed with exercise. Compulsive running is a classic example, in which the runner becomes addicted to the "runner's high" and runs for hours every day, devoting most of his or her free time to achieving higher and higher mileage. Compulsive runners often experience severe discomfort or withdrawal if they have to miss their daily run; their all-consuming compulsion to exercise serves to throw their lives out of balance.

As is the case with all areas of wellness, balance is the key. Choose a form of exercise that you enjoy and stick with it. Make sure that you keep your commitment to exercise within reasonable bounds so that you do not overlook other important aspects of your overall quality of life in recovery.

In chapter 12 you will receive guidance in conducting a quarterly and annual wellness evaluation, to assist you in reevaluating your long-range goals and "raising the bar" on your exercise goals. When you conduct your periodic wellness evaluations, you should consider adding some resistance training to your exercise program. You may also want to enroll in a class in yoga or tai chi sometime in the future.

By now you are beginning to appreciate that wellness is a dynamic process, and that the various elements of a wellness-oriented lifestyle complement each other in a highly synergistic fashion. One of the great benefits of exercise is that it can help us take the edge off the various stresses that we face daily. In the following chapter we take a closer look at the importance of stress management in recovery, together with how we can fine-tune our skills for effectively managing the wide range of stresses we encounter in our day-to-day lives.

Stress Management
and Meditation

Stress is a given in our hectic, modern-day lives. Developing a repertoire of effective stress management skills is critically important during early recovery, as well as in ongoing sobriety maintenance. Equally important, learning how to manage day-to-day stresses effectively is one of the most powerful steps you can take in charting your pathway to optimal health. In this chapter, you will learn how to become a stress survivor and actually thrive in stressful situations.

The Effects of
Excessive Stress on Your Health

While medical science has historically downplayed the role of stress in illness, this posture has shifted dramatically over the past several decades. Many standard medical textbooks now attribute anywhere from 50 to 80 percent of all disease to stress-related origins, and the American Academy of Family Physicians estimates that two-thirds of all office visits to family practitioners are prompted by stress-related symptoms.

Physical illnesses that are increasingly classified as stress-related include heart disease, hypertension, stomach ulcers, ulcerative colitis, bronchial asthma, dermatitis, lower back pain and chronic headaches, to name a few. A growing number of scientists also speculate that an unhealthy stress level may also play a role in the development and progression of various forms of cancer.

Here are some highlights from the growing body of evidence attesting to the detrimental effects of excessive stress on our health:

- **Heart Disease:** In the mid-1970s, cardiologists Ray Rosenman and Meyer Friedman turned the medical world on its head when they released findings of their eight-and-one-half-year study investigating the relationship between hard-driving, stress-prone Type A personalities and the onset of heart disease. Their findings, which focused on 3,524 participants, demonstrated that the incidence of heart disease was twice as high for the Type A study subjects than for their more relaxed Type B counterparts. In a related study, these same cardiologists studied the impact of excessive stress on serum cholesterol levels by observing a group of tax accountants during the tax season. Significantly, as they were bombarded by unrelenting deadline pressures, the accountants registered cholesterol levels as high as 100 points above their normal readings.

- **Sudden Cardiac Death:** Another cardiologist, Peter Reich, examined a sample of one hundred cases of sudden cardiac death drawn from coroner's records. His investigation revealed that almost two-thirds of the victims were under moderate to severe stress on the final day of their life, and that more than one in five were experiencing acute stress during the last thirty minutes of life.

- **Use of Prescription Drugs:** Patterns of prescription drug use among the general population are telling in reference to the detrimental effects of excessive stress on our health. Significantly, the four bestselling groups of drugs in America are ulcer medications, hypertension drugs, tranquilizers and antidepressants.

- **Stress and the Common Cold:** Researchers at the Carnegie Mellon Institute have concluded that excessive stress can increase our susceptibility to colds and the flu. After psychologists assessed the stress level of over 400 healthy adults, subjects were then given nasal drops that contained a small dose of respiratory-disease viruses (talk about a sadistic study design!). Subjects with the highest stress levels ran twice the risk of getting a cold and were five times as likely to become infected with the cold virus.

Beyond a doubt, chronic stress overload is hazardous to your health. As a recovering alcoholic/addict, you are at additional risk from the detrimental effects of stress because they may undermine your recovery program. Let's take a closer look at the critical importance of stress management in relapse prevention.

Role of Stress Management in Relapse Prevention

The 12-step acronym HALT—which is a reminder to the newly sober never to get too **H**ungry, **A**ngry, **L**onely or **T**ired— provides vivid testimony to the crucial importance of avoiding stress overload in safeguarding against relapse. In discussing the role of stress management in relapse prevention, particularly during the critical early stages of recovery, relapse prevention authority Terence Gorski unequivocally states:

> *Learn effective stress-management techniques. Under high stress, the symptoms of post-acute withdrawal get worse. At times of low stress, they get better. Therefore, stress management is important.*

Gorski's sound advice concerning the importance of stress management in relapse prevention is bolstered by scientific research findings.

In 1991, a group of researches focused on 171 male alcoholics who had completed inpatient treatment, hoping to study the possible influence of anxiety in contributing to relapse. Participants were divided into subjects who successfully maintained abstinence following treatment versus those who subsequently relapsed. Applying a battery of psychological tests, investigators were able to track subjects' anxiety levels at various points throughout the study. While both groups registered comparable anxiety scores during the treatment period, following completion of treatment the subjects who successfully stayed clean and sober were found to have significantly lower anxiety scores.

My own research focusing on a group of fifty alcoholics/ addicts completing residential treatment yielded similar results. In my study, subjects were asked to subjectively rate the overall level of stress in their lives and were also questioned about whether they regularly practiced meditation or another form of relaxation. Significantly, a full 40 percent of subjects who relapsed rated the level of stress in their lives as "excessive," compared with only 8 percent of subjects who successfully stayed clean and sober. Furthermore, a full 72 percent of subjects in the successful recovery group reported that they practiced a daily relaxation ritual, compared with only 28 percent of subjects who relapsed. Together, these findings confirm the importance of stress management in safeguarding against relapse.

Highly stressful events, such as the tragic attacks of September 11, 2001, severely test our mettle and are associated with increased likelihood of relapse. Terence Gorski observes that the months following September 11 were accompanied by increased alcohol/drug consumption and relapse, as reported by treatment centers across the country. Significantly, many recovering alcoholics and addicts who successfully maintained sobriety throughout this difficult period continued to regularly attend their 12-step meetings, while practicing the various stress management skills outlined in this chapter.

Let's move on to the practical applications of stress management skills in your daily life.

Practical Applications:
How to Become a Stress Survivor

Another reason that learning effective stress management skills is vitally important to you and your loved ones is that addictive behavior is often a misguided effort to manage day-to-day stress. What you want to aim for, instead, is to be a "stress survivor."

In learning how to become a stress survivor, we must first discard the notion that all stress is inherently bad. As shown in the illustration of the Stress-Performance Curve, the presence of a moderate level of stress in our lives is healthy and even welcome. It motivates us to be fully alive and to strive for optimal performance. Indeed, one of the essential principles of effective stress management is to maintain an optimal level of stress—as represented by the midpoint in the Stress-Performance Curve. Unfortunately, most of us suffer from stress overload a good deal of the time, and we need to work at achieving a better balance. In fact, if we're not careful we can even become "adrenaline junkies," addicted to living on the edge. (See sidebar, p. 111.)

Stress-Performance Curve

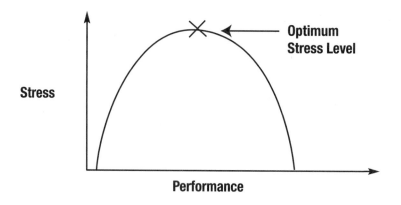

Are You an Adrenaline Junkie?

Many (if not most) people with addictive disorders crave excitement and feel a need to "live on the edge" at all times—even after they have entered recovery. Examples of hard-core "adrenaline junkies" that I have personally witnessed include recovering alcoholics who take jobs as bartenders and recovering people who literally become addicted to reckless driving at excessive speeds.

Adrenaline junkies tend to be attracted to high-pressure jobs and professions. They often seem to create an endless series of crises in their lives in order to avoid slowing down and facing who they really are. They also experience great difficulty in setting appropriate boundaries between their work and family lives, to the dismay of their spouses and children. They tend to be attracted to risky behaviors of all sorts—compulsive gambling, skydiving, hang gliding and risky romantic liaisons, for example—anything and everything to keep the adrenaline rushing through their systems.

Being an adrenaline junkie is extremely disruptive to your serenity and hazardous to your long-term sobriety. In addition, it poses serious risks to your mental, emotional and physical well-being. To be honest, we are all adrenaline junkies at one level or another—it's really a matter of degree. The following tips are offered to help you break this cycle.

- **Listen to your body:** Tune in to your body's signals that indicate stress is building—and do something to break the cycle. Try deep breathing and/or taking a short "time out" from a highly stressful situation to bring yourself back to center. Regular physical exercise is by far the best stress-buster available to most of us.

> • **Remember that *balance* is the key:** Set reasonable limits on your work-related expectations and energy expenditure, and strive to balance your work with healthy doses of rest and recreation. As Rick Carlson says in his classic bestseller *Don't Sweat the Small Stuff,* we all need to remember that when we die, our in-box will still be full!
> • **Practice the Serenity Prayer (see page 114):** Remind yourself constantly that "life is not an emergency," and there is only so much that you can change or control.

In short, overstress is a lack of balance between the demands that life places on us and our resources for coping with them. We can strive to achieve a better balance—either by addressing the problem at its core by reducing the major sources of stress in our lives, or by strengthening our internal and external coping tools. Usually, we need to attack the problem along both fronts.

Wellness Pointers for Stress Management

A wellness-oriented lifestyle serves as an effective buffer against stress overload in many ways. Regular vigorous exercise, for example, strengthens our heart-lung capacity, channeling oxygen throughout the body, which enables us to calm down and return to normal more rapidly when we experience stressful situations. At the same time, exercise provides an extremely powerful method for *discharging* accumulated stress from our body.

Likewise, by bringing our diets into balance, we are feeding the cells and tissues of our body with "high octane fuel," thus enabling our central nervous system and other body systems to respond effectively to whatever challenges face us. As discussed in chapter 5, it is particularly important to minimize our intake of "nutritional stressors," including caffeine, sugar, white flour products and high-fat foods. Additional components of a wellness-oriented lifestyle include: striking a wholesome balance between work, rest and recreation; enjoying the many benefits of a strong social support system; and living in attunement with our spiritual essence. Together, they enhance our ability to manage day-to-day stress.

The following wellness pointers include some practical stress management strategies I have learned over the years. You may wish to consider incorporating some of these tools into your own stress management program:

- Practice the Serenity Prayer throughout the day (see page 114). In my opinion, this is the most powerful stress management tool available.
- Learn the art of self-nurturance, practice giving and receiving positive "strokes," and get (and give) at least five hugs a day!
- Set aside a daily mind-quieting period for meditation, prayer, listening to relaxing music or just sitting quietly.
- Recognize that clear and harmonious communications are essential to stress reduction and sobriety maintenance, as most stress arises from lack of harmony in our communications with others.
- Learn the art of time management and avoid overscheduling yourself. Consciously schedule "slack time" into your daily routine.
- Be sure to get seven to eight hours of sleep each night. If you suffer from insomnia, ask yourself if you are consuming too

much caffeine or sugar. Take a warm bath, or choose another activity, to relax yourself before going to bed. (See the sidebar on pages 14–15—"A Simple Self-Hypnosis Exercise to Ease You into a Relaxing Sleep.")

- Practice deep breathing, especially when confronted with highly stressful situations. Take a moment to pause, take a few deep breaths and bring yourself back to center. (See the sidebar on pages 13–14—"Stress-Buster Deep Breathing Exercise.")

- Treat yourself to a massage. Massage can work wonders in terms of releasing accumulated stress from our muscles. Nothing beats getting (or giving) a good massage!

- Learn to laugh at yourself and defuse stressful situations with humor. Back in high school, one of my old buddies used to tell me, "Don't take life so seriously. You'll never get out alive anyhow!"

Now let's move on to a detailed discussion of two powerful stress management tools—following the Serenity Prayer and practicing daily meditation or another mind-quieting ritual.

The Serenity Prayer as a Stress Management Tool

The Serenity Prayer

God grant me the serenity to accept the things I cannot change,
courage to change the things I can
and wisdom to know the difference.

In terms of stress management, the Serenity Prayer says it all! I became intimately familiar with the power of the Serenity Prayer one morning a little over ten years ago, when I was at an extremely stressful juncture in my life.

At the time, I was working as community outreach coordinator for an acute psychiatric hospital. While the pay was nothing to write home about, the work was extremely gratifying. I traveled widely throughout our part of Southern California, giving talks on substance abuse prevention and rehabilitation to schools, employee assistance programs and other potential referral sources for our hospital. I also gave talks to inmates at a local prison as part of their pre-release program, coordinated our annual Red Ribbon Week outreach to the public schools, led a weekly wellness group for our adult patients and derived tremendous gratification from my connections with the recovery community.

At the same time, I was experiencing a heavy overload of stress in my life. I was acutely aware that our parent company was totally bottom-line oriented, and that our hospital's occupancy level had dropped to an all-time low, due to cutbacks mandated by managed care. I had two mortgages on our home, and I was angry and despondent over the fact that I had no job security—despite having been a loyal and dedicated employee for over three years.

One Saturday morning it all "hit the fan" when I opened a notice from the IRS. They informed me that I owed several thousand dollars in back taxes, interest and penalties because I had failed to withhold Social Security contributions from my earnings as a freelance consultant a number of years earlier. I walked down to the street below, sat by the curb and thought about how easy it would be to just run out into the oncoming traffic and put an end to my misery. My wife was understandably very frightened by my behavior. She called 911 and a couple of police officers came out to "talk me down."

This episode drove home to me, very powerfully, the need to practice the Serenity Prayer on a daily basis. Focusing on the prayer, I began to reflect on my need to accept the momentary realities associated with my unstable employment situation. At the same time, I also needed to accept that this did not negate the many, many precious things in my life: my loving wife, stepchildren and grandchildren; my love for the guitar and folk singing; and the intense pleasure I derive from my creative writing, among other things. I then turned my attention to the courage part of the prayer and began to reflect on the need to actively focus my attention on lining up a more secure job— even though I was understandably reluctant to let go of the aspects of my present job that I found intrinsically rewarding.

The Serenity Prayer has literally saved my life on more than one occasion. Today, I carry a copy of the prayer in my wallet as a constant reminder. I also have a framed copy in my bedroom and keep a copy posted in my office at work.

Now I would like to share with you a worksheet I have developed for using the Serenity Prayer as a stress management tool.

Serenity Prayer Stress Management Worksheet

God grant me the serenity to accept the things I cannot change,
courage to change the things I can
and wisdom to know the difference.

Identification: Identify a troublesome problem in your life. Describe the situation and how it affects you.

_____

_____

_____

_____

Acceptance: List those aspects of the situation that are beyond your power to change or influence (at least at the moment).

_____

_____

_____

_____

Courage: List those aspects of the situation that you can begin to work on changing or influencing, together with any ideas that come to mind about how you might go about making these changes.

_____

_____

_____

_____

How to Use the Serenity Prayer Worksheet

I would encourage you to take a few minutes to practice using the Serenity Prayer worksheet as a tool for getting a better handle on stressful situations. (Before doing this, you may want to make several copies of the worksheet for future use.)

When I feel overwhelmed by stresses in my life and attempt to calm myself down, I find this worksheet extremely helpful. By using this structured format to put everything down in writing, I find that I can better sort things out and be more objective about how to best focus my energies. Invariably, I discover that one of the essential elements I need to work on changing is my *attitude* toward the situation that I perceive as being so inherently stressful and unfair. Taking this exercise one step further, you may also wish to get some additional opinions and perspective on your problem by discussing your answers with your partner, your sponsor or someone else in whom you place a great deal of trust.

Practicing a Daily Mind-Quieting Ritual

In addition to practicing the Serenity Prayer and using the Serenity Prayer worksheet, you can also take the edge off day-to-day stresses by incorporating meditation or another mind-quieting ritual into your daily routine.

Before discussing potential applications of meditation, we should take a moment to clear up some common misconceptions regarding this term. Meditation is simply a natural process of relaxing and clearing the mind. If you have ever been awestruck by a beautiful sunset or felt at one with the world while hiking in nature, you have experienced a meditative state. While many people use prayer as a form of meditating, meditation does not need to be associated with any particular religious or spiritual practice.

Now, let's focus for a moment on some evidence concerning the many benefits associated with meditation in terms of stress reduction. Dr. Herbert Benson, associate professor of medicine at the Harvard Medical School and founder and president of the Mind/Body Medical Institute, conducted extensive, groundbreaking research in this area. Some of the highlights of this research by Benson and his associates are listed below:

- Patients with hypertension who practiced meditation experienced significant decreases in blood pressure and a reduced need for medications over a three-year follow-up period.
- Seventy-five percent of patients with insomnia who were taught a simple form of meditation were cured and became normal sleepers.
- People suffering from migraine and cluster headaches who began to meditate found they had fewer and less severe headaches.
- Patients suffering from chronic pain reported less severity of pain, more activity, less anxiety and fewer visits to doctors after they began practicing medication.

In 1991, a team of social scientists conducted an overview of twenty-four studies designed to examine the potential benefits of meditation in both prevention and treatment of substance abuse. Collectively, the findings from these studies documented a reduced use of alcohol and drugs, increased abstinence, and reduced rates of relapse among subjects who regularly practiced meditation. The researchers concluded that meditation appears to offer a natural alternative to substance abuse by providing participants with relief from anxiety, enhanced self-esteem and an increased sense of power and control over their lives.

Why is meditation so effective as a stress reduction tool? To answer this question, we first need to focus on what takes place in our bodies when we experience stress.

The Flight or Fight Response

Since prehistoric times, our bodies have been programmed to react automatically to situations that we perceive as stressful by means of what is commonly called the "flight or fight" response. Whenever a situation appears to represent an immediate threat, our brain instantly triggers the release of adrenaline into our bloodstream. This, in turn, triggers a variety of physiological responses designed to get our bodies into a state of "combat readiness." Among other things, we experience increases in our heart rate, respiration and blood pressure; the muscles throughout our body begin to tighten; and our digestive system shuts down, allowing the body to focus its energies more fully on responding to the crisis at hand.

In prehistoric times, when many of our stresses were associated with imminent physical danger, these mechanisms served us well. We would respond to the immediate crisis, and when it was over our bodily systems returned to normal. In today's world, however, we are typically confronted with a constant barrage of major to minor "hassles" that generally cannot be resolved immediately. Our physiological programming has not changed, however, and our bodies still kick in with the flight or fight response. Consequently, far too many of us walk around in a constant state of "combat alertness." Over time, this can take a serious toll on both our physical health and our mental/emotional well-being. Additionally, this "combat state" seriously disrupts our relationships with family, friends and coworkers.

In contrast to the flight or fight response, which forms our bodies' natural response to stress, practicing one of the many forms of meditation serves to program us for a "relaxation response"—which helps return both our minds and bodies to their natural state of rest and calm.

There are many forms of meditation available. Some of the more popular forms include:

- Transcendental meditation and similar techniques that employ repetition of a "mantra," or neutral word, to help quiet the mind
- Zen-based meditation, and other forms of meditation that involve focusing attention on the breath
- Movement meditations, including yoga, tai chi and Sufi dancing
- Contemplative prayer

The goal of all meditative practices is similar—to quiet our minds and get more closely in touch with the center of our being. I have personally practiced transcendental meditation twice a day for the past twenty-five years and find it very helpful as both a calming and a centering experience. Rather than recommending any particular form of meditation, however, I would simply urge you to familiarize yourself with the various approaches and choose the path that represents the best fit for you.

Incidentally, you do not need to practice a formally structured meditation technique to gain the benefits associated with a daily mind-quieting period. Other useful daily relaxation rituals might include watching the sunset, listening to relaxing music or meditation tapes, or taking a contemplative walk through your neighborhood at the beginning of the day.

A Simple, Mind-Quieting Meditation Exercise

Here is a simple, mind-quieting exercise that is very similar to the popular transcendental meditation program. If you are not already practicing meditation, you may wish to experiment with this technique.

1. Sit in a comfortable chair with good back support. Make sure you will not be disturbed for the duration of this exercise.
2. Close your eyes. Let your breathing become slow and natural.
3. Begin silently repeating the word "one." Keep repeating the word "one" over and over, throughout this exercise. As you become aware of other thoughts or feelings, simply let go of them and bring your awareness back to repeating the word "one."
4. After anywhere between ten and twenty minutes of meditating, stop repeating the word "one" and gradually bring your awareness back to your immediate surroundings. Take a minute or two to do this. Then open your eyes, get up and go about your business.

For the sake of illustration, I chose the word "one" as a point of focus because it is a neutral sounding term. You may use any neutral sounding term that you prefer.

Your meditation sessions should run anywhere between ten and twenty minutes, depending on what is comfortable for you. When you feel that you have been meditating for the allotted period, you may glance at your watch to check the time. If your time is not yet up, close your eyes and continue to meditate. With practice, you will begin to develop a good feel for how long you have been meditating.

To derive maximum benefit from this simple meditation exercise, you should practice it twice a day—in the morning right before breakfast and in the evening before supper. If twice a day seems too much, begin by practicing this exercise once a day at a designated time. The important thing is to be consistent and practice whatever mind-quieting ritual you choose to follow on a daily basis.

Throughout this chapter, I have introduced you to a variety of stress-management techniques and strategies that you can begin to incorporate into your quest for high-level wellness. Another powerful way to cope effectively with day-to-day stresses is to enjoy the benefits associated with a strong network of supportive friends and family. This topic forms the focus of the following chapter.

Developing a Strong Social Support System

Just as we nourish our bodies with the foods we eat, we nurture our souls and psyches with the quality of our relationships. In this chapter, we examine the critical importance of social relationships in supporting our commitment to sobriety and fostering overall health and well-being.

Nurturing Relationships for Our Health and Well-Being

Mountains of evidence suggest that positive relationships with family, friends and coworkers can actually help us live longer and enjoy a positive state of health. The landmark *Surgeon General's Report on Health Promotion and Disease Prevention,* issued over two decades ago, unequivocally states that a positive social support system can play a major role in modifying the harmful effects of stress; aid in recovery from surgery, heart disease and infectious diseases; and serve as a valuable safeguard against depression when we are faced with adversity.

A classic study focusing on residents of Alameda County, California, which tracked the health status of over 7,000 adults over a nine-year period, provides striking evidence concerning the health benefits of positive relationships with other people. Significantly, subjects who were classified as lonely or isolated experienced death rates three times higher than did subjects who reported stronger social ties. A similar study, which followed 2,754 adults in Tecumseh, Michigan, over a ten-year period, also demonstrated that subjects with active social networks had the best health. In this study, the most socially isolated subjects had four times the mortality rate of those who enjoyed strong support systems. Simply put, people with an active network of friends and family tend to live longer and enjoy a more healthy life.

Available evidence also suggests that when we are sick, our chances of experiencing a positive healing outcome are dramatically increased when we have the benefits of a strong support system. One study, which focused on 2,500 elderly men and women, provides compelling evidence concerning the positive influence that friends and family can have in promoting healing from a heart attack. Among participants who were hospitalized for heart attacks during the study, the subjects with the strongest support systems had by far the best survival experience. Significantly, only 12 percent of subjects reporting two or more sources of social support died while in the hospital—compared with 23 percent of subjects reporting only one source of social support and a full 38 percent of subjects who reported no close friends or family ties.

Interestingly, a number of studies have also documented improved immune system functioning among people with strong social supports—suggesting that positive relationships may even promote increased resistance to colds and flu.

How does the state of matrimony influence our overall state of health? Contrary to what the skeptics might have you believe, numerous studies have documented that as a group, married people tend to fare better than their unmarried counterparts in terms of enjoying positive health. A nationwide survey conducted by the National Center for Health Statistics, involving 122,859 people in 47,240 families, demonstrated that across the board, married people reported fewer health problems than unmarried people did. Statistically, married men outlive bachelors by close to ten years. Regarding heart disease, our nation's leading killer, the likelihood of contracting heart disease is twice as high for divorcees than for people who are married. Numerous studies have suggested that marriage may also confer a protective influence against cancer, in that married people have a lower incidence of many types of cancer. In addition, when cancer does strike, married patients are more likely to survive.

In summary, the evidence suggests that positive relationships with other people confer very powerful benefits relating to both health and longevity.

The Value of Relationships in Maintaining Sobriety and Preventing Relapse

Available evidence provides strong support for the conventional wisdom held by treatment professionals: a strong, recovery-focused support system is critically important in promoting long-term sobriety. Clearly, such a support system is vital during early sobriety, when you are exceptionally vulnerable to a million and one influences that may trigger a craving for a drink or drug. Once you have successfully navigated the early stages of recovery, the bonds that you maintain with fellow 12-steppers—or members of your chosen recovery program—remain the bedrock of your foundation for lasting sobriety.

The connection between active participation in 12-step meetings and successfully maintaining sobriety was strikingly borne out by findings of my own research, which compared recovering alcoholics/addicts who successfully stayed clean and sober with a similar group of subjects who suffered a major relapse. Significantly, a full 88 percent of the clean and sober subjects reported that they attended 12-step meetings at least once a week, compared with only 36 percent of subjects in the relapse group.

Above and beyond 12-step program participation, numerous studies also suggest that positive relations with friends and family can contribute to successful sobriety maintenance. One study examined 392 alcoholic patients undergoing treatment, with particular reference to their marital status. The researchers found that married subjects tended to fare better in treatment, registering higher scores in terms of psychological well-being and self-esteem, while perceiving their drinking as being less problematic.

Findings of another study conducted at the VA hospital in San

Diego suggest that a strong support system provides valuable assistance in safeguarding against relapse, even when one is confronted with an unusually high level of stress. Study subjects were recovering alcoholics who had recently experienced highly stressful events, such as divorce, loss of employment or serious illness. Significantly, the researchers discovered that the subjects who reported strong social support networks fared better in terms of ongoing sobriety maintenance, despite the presence of major stressors in their lives.

More recently, subjects in my own research were asked to rate their level of satisfaction with their relationships with family and friends. Significantly, a full 52 percent of the clean and sober subjects reported that they were very satisfied with these relationships, compared with only 16 percent of the subjects who relapsed.

Taken together, available evidence suggests that maintaining healthy relationships with family, friends and coworkers can be of major assistance in promoting long-term sobriety and safeguarding against relapse.

Developing Support Systems for Wellness and Recovery

The following suggestions will help you develop an effective support system that is an integral component of your journey to wellness and recovery.

Go to Meetings

It goes without saying that ongoing participation in 12-step meetings or another recovery-focused support group is essential to maintaining sobriety and growing in recovery. A wellness-oriented lifestyle and working your program definitely go hand in hand. Clearly, your active participation in 12-step meetings and the bond of friendship with other people in recovery can serve as a powerful lifeline in securing your sobriety, one day at a time. In addition, the support and acceptance that recovery-focused meetings afford both newcomers and old-timers alike serves as a valuable safe harbor—providing the freedom and security that will enable you to reach out to other people and share those aspects of your background that you had previously swept under the rug. These are invaluable social skills. You can use them in other areas of your life to reap the full benefits of mutually trusting friendships with all kinds of people.

Broaden Your Social Support Network

To gain the full benefits of a strong group of friends and acquaintances that fully support your commitment to wellness, I encourage you to broaden your social support network. Get involved in social activities that will connect you with other health conscious people. If you like outdoor activities, join a local hiking or biking club and partake in the wonders of nature with other like-minded souls. If you are finding it difficult to stick with a regular exercise program, consider joining a walking club or signing up with a conditioning class at your local community college. Likewise, if you want to lose some weight, consider joining Weight Watchers or another weight-loss support group.

In many respects, we live in a society that is both isolating and depersonalizing at many levels. We all yearn for a sense of community that supports our unique core values and our need for social connection. Finding this in the midst of today's fast-paced world can be a major challenge. We need to seek out meaningful outlets that allow us to channel our energies into things that excite us and causes we believe in, and that enable us to connect with others who share our sense of excitement and enthusiasm. Look for organizations focusing on special interests that intrigue you—volunteer to spend part of your time helping others in a spirit of loving service, or consider becoming politically involved in furthering a cause that you passionately support—whatever that may be. Be creative! For example, if your particular pet cause doesn't have an organization or office in your community, consider rolling up your sleeves and organizing a group yourself.

Address Issues Within Your Family System

Our family relationships provide us with especially meaningful opportunities for giving and receiving love and experiencing mutual support. Many people in recovery, however, come from highly dysfunctional families. As Claudia Black vividly illustrates in her classic bestseller focusing on adult children of alcoholics— *It Will Never Happen To Me!*—this pattern can perpetuate itself through many generations unless we take conscious action to break the vicious cycle.

Knowing that we live in families that are far from perfect, we must learn to set appropriate limits on our interactions with certain family members so we don't become drained or overwhelmed. The holiday season can be particularly stressful, since it seems to bring out the best and the worst in family dynamics. Simply being aware of this reality can help us focus on what we need to do to take care of ourselves during family gatherings that may carry highly stressful overtones. (For a look at the lighter side of our dysfunctional family backgrounds, see the sidebar "Putting the Fun Back into Dysfunction.")

Family relationships can be a double-edged sword for people in the early stages of recovery. When a former alcoholic/addict enters recovery, it often poses serious challenges to pre-existing dynamics within the family system. Indeed, the newly recovering person's spouse, parents and even children may have a personal stake in keeping things as they were. Oftentimes, family members are not consciously aware of their resistance to the changes accompanying the recovering person's new sobriety.

Open and caring dialogue is essential to nurturing family dynamics that are supportive of the recovering person's commitment to sobriety. This underscores the critical importance of family involvement in both primary treatment and continuing care. If particularly troublesome family issues begin to surface, a structured approach to family therapy may be needed. Involving the entire family in therapy with a professional who is grounded in principles of recovery can be extremely beneficial in helping the family attain a new state of positive equilibrium.

Putting the Fun Back into Dysfunction

Let's face it—we all come from dysfunctional families, and we all have our share of idiosyncrasies that would put Woody Allen to shame if these inner quirks were fully exposed to the outside world. Learning to laugh at ourselves and the more absurd sides of our nature can go a long way towards learning to cope with those aspects of ourselves and our lives that are far less than perfect.

As the story goes, several years ago a team of New Age entrepreneurs dreamed up the idea of hosting a national conference centered on the theme of "Adult Children from Normal, Healthy Families." They spent millions of dollars on an intensive promotional splash, and the conference was a complete flop—as nobody came. Apparently, no one felt that he or she met the criteria for membership in this extremely elite group!

Many people would claim that Southern California, my adopted homeland, is the nation's capital of dysfunction. After all, we invented the 70 percent divorce rate, which the rest of the nation has long since embraced, and while New Yorkers point with pride to the Empire State Building and Parisians boast the Eiffel Tower, our own signature landmark is Disneyland, with the "Hollywood Sign" running a close second. And yours truly is living proof of the old adage that if the country were stood on its edge, everything loose would come rolling down into California!

Some of my favorite spoofs relating to California, as well as to the dysfunctional sides of our natures, include:

- You know you're from California when you insist that your therapist and Co-Dependents Anonymous (CODA) sponsor accompany you to all your family gatherings, just to be on the safe side.

- You know you're from California when you cruise the singles haunts making up stories of your two failed marriages just to fit in—although you've been single all your life.

- And Woody Allen's classic line—"Of course I'm screwed up— I came from a completely dysfunctional family where my parents had nothing in common. They were even of the opposite sex!"

Form Meaningful Relationships and Avoid Toxic People

In order to form truly meaningful relationships with other people, we need to risk disclosing who we really are. We need to overcome our fear of rejection in order to reach out and connect with our fellow travelers on this planet. We also need to exercise discretion in choosing whom to trust and avoid "slippery places and slippery faces." We need to learn to avoid "toxic people" or energy drainers—and consciously seek out people who, by their very presence, are genuinely uplifting and provide an instant "energy boost."

Learn to validate the positive attributes of family, friends, coworkers—everyone around you—and go out of your way to spend quality time with people who validate your own good qualities and the dreams to which you aspire.

Many of us also need to make a special effort to validate our intrinsic worthiness. This allows us to reach out to people with whom we would truly like to connect. Otherwise, we risk constantly replaying the punch line from the old Groucho Marx joke, "I don't want to belong to any club that will accept me as a member."

Expressing Your Sexuality in Recovery

Our discussion of the value of intimacy and social relationships in wellness and recovery would be incomplete if we failed to address this vitally important, yet often overlooked, dimension of recovery.

Many people experience a good deal of awkwardness in attempting to express and fully enjoy the sexual side of their

nature during the early stages of recovery. This may be particularly true if in the past we relied excessively on alcohol, mari-
juana, cocaine, ecstasy or other drugs as a prelude to connecting
with sexually attractive people and "getting it on."

When we were drinking and using, we may have tended to
rush headlong into lustful sexual encounters fueled by momentary passion, forgoing the stages of friendship, bonding and
forming mutual trust that precede the expression of sexual intimacy in a mature and healthy relationship. As is true with so
many aspects of recovery, we need to learn to slow down, get off
the roller coaster and simply take it one step at a time.

Even in the context of a caring and intimate relationship,
many people in recovery experience a certain degree of awkwardness regarding the physical expression of sexual intimacy
without the "instant aphrodisiac" that booze and drugs may have
formerly provided.

To experience the full richness of physical sexual expression in
recovery, we need to shift our focus and cultivate an appreciation
for a relaxed, non-goal-oriented approach to sexual expression.
That expression is appropriately focused on the here and now,
and grounded in mutual trust and understanding. Unfortunately, this is often easier said than done. In our goal-oriented
society, we all too often feel compelled to jump into bed with
our partner and rush headlong into orgasm. This can be particularly problematic for men, as we tend to be extremely goal-
oriented and defensive about our sexual expression.

Women, of course, have their own issues regarding healthy
expression of their sexuality in recovery. This is especially true for
the many women in recovery who were victimized in abusive
relationships going back to their families of origin, as well as

during their former drinking and drugging days.

One of the lessons I have learned in my own therapy is that there are many different pathways to making love with our chosen partner, which include, but also extend beyond, the act of physical connection. These may include treasuring the sound of our partner's voice, honoring his or her many moods, and cherishing and nurturing our partner with love and affection as we travel through life together. In terms of our physical expression of sexual intimacy, rather than approaching our lovemaking as an obsessive rush to attain orgasm, it is much wiser (and more fun) to simply allow ourselves to relax with our partner and focus our attention on *enjoying the journey*. We need to learn to fully embrace and enjoy this intimate journey, regardless of where it may or may not take us in a particular lovemaking encounter.

Many psychotherapists who work with couples having trouble in this area encourage them to engage for several weeks in a process called "sensate focusing." During this process, the couple explicitly agrees to make love *without* the goal of copulation and orgasm. Simply put, sensate focusing involves simply lying with our partner, cuddling and caressing them in whatever way we find pleasurable, and focusing our full attention on just enjoying these sensations to the fullest in a relaxed manner. Try it—it can be a real turn-on! One of my own favorite books on this subject is *The Art of Sexual Ecstasy*, by Margo Anand. Emmett Miller has also developed an excellent audiocassette addressing this theme, titled *Sexual Intimacy*.

Suggestions for the
Single Person in Recovery

Addressing the special issues faced by single people in recovery is particularly important because chemical dependency has been correctly defined as a disease of loneliness.

Early in recovery, we tend to be particularly shaky and vulnerable, as our bodies and psyches are undergoing a major readjustment that takes many months—often years—to work itself out. In recognition of the very vulnerable status of alcoholics and addicts during the early stages of recovery, AA and other 12-step programs wisely discourage forming sponsorship relations with persons of the opposite sex, and also caution against emotional entanglements early on.

The following are offered as some practical pointers for surviving and thriving as a single person in recovery:

- First, recognize that although you are single, you do not need to be alone. Becoming actively involved in your 12-step program, going to meetings, working with your sponsor and eventually offering to sponsor someone else when you are ready, all provide excellent opportunities for reaching out socially to others in recovery and fending off loneliness and isolation.

- Nurture a sincere appreciation of the importance of forming wholesome relationships with persons of both sexes and seek out people who share your core values and basic interests.

- In particular, be on guard against the traps and pitfalls associated with addictive relationships. When we perceive ourselves as being incomplete, it is easy to fall into the trap of seeking a partner who will validate us and make us feel whole. When we become embroiled in relationship addictions, we tend to carry this pattern to an unhealthy extreme. This invariably places an excessive burden on the other person in the relationship and can even jeopardize our sobriety.

My own experience as a divorced single during my thirties and early forties vividly illustrates the dangers associated with relationship addictions. When my first marriage ended, I was twenty-nine and my self-esteem was at an all-time low. I was caught up in a vicious cycle of self-loathing and worthlessness. In an effort to escape my emotional pain, I became enmeshed in a self-destructive pattern of addictive relationships that lasted for over ten years. Invariably, I would rush into relationships with the wrong women, attracted to these liaisons by the initial sexual intensity. I would push for intimacy and commitment before my partner was ready (out of my feelings of insecurity and my intense need for external validation), and invariably I ended up getting hurt. It took me many years of work in therapy to finally "get it," and to begin to develop an appreciation of the need to *slow down*. I also had to do some major work on learning how to validate my own worth as a person—rather than burdening my partner with unreasonable expectations that she do it for me.

In truth, our most important relationship is with ourselves, and we need to get that one down first! Once you have reached a level of growth where you are truly comfortable with yourself as a whole person, then—and only then—will you be ready to attract into your life a truly meaningful, mutually nourishing relationship with long-term potential.

Throughout this chapter, we have developed the theme that positive relationships can have an extremely beneficial effect on our overall state of health and well-being, in addition to anchoring us in our sobriety. The key to creating and maintaining a strong social support system lies in the ability to develop loving and trusting relationships with other people, characterized by mutual caring and respect. Let's move on to the next chapter, which focuses on the spiritual dimension of recovery, with particular reference to the importance of creating meaning and fulfillment in our lives.

CHAPTER

9

Cultivating Your Central Purpose, Spirituality and Life Satisfaction

This chapter addresses the critically important interconnection between your central purpose (your unique calling in life), spirituality and life satisfaction. These three personal dimensions are important cornerstones of your wellness and recovery program.

Cultivating Your Unique Central Purpose

I earnestly hope that you will become passionately involved in discovering your unique sense of purpose. To assist you with this process, I'll present a series of exercises to guide you in your personal quest.

Manifesting our unique sense of purpose is the core dimension of wellness, from which all else flows. When we are living in attunement with our sense of destiny, we are intrinsically motivated to take care of ourselves by choosing behaviors and relationships that are truly prolife and prohealth. At the intuitive level, I believe that the very cells and organs of our bodies respond in a positive manner to a consciousness finely attuned to one's calling.

I have always been fascinated by the fact that throughout history, famous inventors, authors, composers and other people whose lives were characterized by an overriding sense of purpose have consistently enjoyed life spans far in excess of those experienced by their contemporaries. Look at the obituaries in your local paper. You will frequently find reports of people who have left their mark on the world and lived far into their eighties, nineties and, not uncommonly, even into their hundreds—despite the fact that the current average life expectancy at birth hovers around the midseventies. In my opinion, this is not coincidental. When we are truly "doing our thing," and wake up every morning expecting to fill our day with meaningful and rewarding activities, our bodies respond positively to this life-affirming message. In truth, I believe that the royal road to longevity lies in living in attunement with our unique sense of purpose for being on this planet.

Cultivating Spirituality

I like to define spirituality as a sense of connection with something greater than ourselves. This can be a feeling of connection with a higher power, a sense of being part of a universal life force, a feeling of being in flow with life, a sense of attunement with the natural rhythms of the universe, or all of the above—and infinitely more. We live and breath our spirituality when we are pursuing a mission that is greater than ourselves. When you truly believe that your life is filled with purpose and you have precious gifts to offer, you will be strongly motivated to work your chosen recovery program and experience the full benefits of sobriety. It is no coincidence that the spiritual dimension of recovery forms the bedrock of Alcoholics Anonymous (AA) and all other 12-step programs.

Cultivating Life Satisfaction

Closely intertwined with the spiritual dimension of recovery is the concept of life satisfaction. In the classic text *Relapse Prevention,* G. Alan Marlatt expounds on the critical importance of striking a positive balance between those activities in our lives that provide us with a sense of intrinsic pleasure or self-fulfillment (the *wants*), versus those activities that we perform out of a sense of obligation (the *shoulds*). Marlatt coins the term *want-should balance* to characterize the degree to which we are able to strike a positive balance between the *wants* and the *shoulds* in our lives.

An example of a *should* that most of us can relate to is the need to earn a living. In our materialistic society, the need to make a living may motivate us to choose employment out of monetary considerations alone, rather than trying to achieve a sense of balance by seeking work that covers our basic expenses while also affording us a sense of self-fulfillment.

Marlatt observes that the *wants* and the *shoulds* are seriously imbalanced in the lives of many, if not most, chemically dependent people. He goes on to observe that a lifestyle characterized by a preponderance of *shoulds* (such as feeling tied to unfulfilling work, or attempting to cope with an emotionally barren relationship) is associated with a sense of self-deprivation. This feeling is invariably accompanied by a corresponding need for self-indulgence. Marlatt views the lives of many alcoholics and addicts as containing an overload of *shoulds,* in which the only breaks and uplifts are provided by overindulgence in alcohol and drugs. This chemical overindulgence gives the user "permission" to engage in other forms of self-indulgent behavior.

In recovery from chemical dependency or other addictive disorders, it is critically important to attain a sense of balance between the *wants* and the *shoulds* in our lives. A wellness-oriented lifestyle can assist you by introducing you to new and rewarding activities—engaging in vigorous exercise, eating wholesome and delicious foods, practicing meditation, and creating mutually rewarding social relationships. Significantly, life satisfaction is intimately tied to the spiritual dimension of recovery, because being genuinely satisfied with our lives is inseparable from finding and expressing our core values and sense of purpose.

Practical Applications

The balance of this chapter presents practical suggestions to help you embrace the spiritual dimension of wellness and recovery through manifesting your unique sense of purpose and creating a truly fulfilling life. These guidelines are suggestive—I encourage you to pursue these suggestions and any other resources that you find particularly helpful in your journey.

Defining Your Central Purpose:
Questions for Reflection

I would like to begin this section by posing several questions for self-reflection. Please be aware that there are no right or wrong answers. These questions are simply presented as possible starting points for your own process of self-discovery:

1. Have you identified your unique sense of purpose in life—that is, a central focus that gives you an ongoing sense of fulfillment in being on this planet and contributes to a high level of enthusiasm for being alive?

2. If your answer to the first question is anything less than a resounding yes, what steps are you willing to take towards identifying and manifesting a central purpose that will bring a profound sense of meaning to your life?

3. Are you fully satisfied with what you are presently doing in the area of career involvement? If not, would you like to make a change—*and* are you willing to *risk* a change?

4. Is your present support system (family, friends, coworkers and other significant people in your life) fully supportive of your pursuing those areas that you believe will be most fulfilling for you?

Again, I encourage you to reflect on your answers to these questions as they "ring true" at this point in your life. You may wish to jot down your responses and refer to them later as you venture along your own chosen pathway.

Some Exercises to Help You Uncover Your Unique Sense of Purpose

The following exercises are designed to assist you in actively exploring steps that you may want to take toward uncovering and manifesting your unique purpose for being on this earth. In posing these suggestions, I have drawn upon some techniques and strategies that I have found to be particularly helpful in my own ongoing quest.

Retreat into Nature and Do Some Soul-Searching

This one holds special meaning for me as I feel most at home when I am in nature—walking along the ocean, hiking in the desert or climbing a mountain peak. Invariably, I find that escaping into nature helps me burn off the stresses and distractions cluttering up my head and get more in touch with what my heart is trying to tell me.

If you can take a weekend retreat to a cabin in the mountains (or wherever)—great! If not, take a mini-retreat to some natural space that holds special meaning for you. This might be a nearby hill, valley, canyon or seashore, or even a park in the middle of the city. When I first moved to Southern California many years ago, I spent countless hours in the hills of Hollywood, looking down over the city and reflecting on where I was going with my life.

Take a notepad with you, get still and quiet, and spend time doing some creative soul-searching and listening to your heart. To assist you in this process, you may consider reflecting on the following questions:

- What would you really like to do with the rest of your life, if you had all the money you will ever need? (In other words, what would you really like to be doing if money were no object?)
- What were your favorite courses in school (not necessarily the ones you got the best grades in), what are your favorite hobbies or pastimes, and what do these things tell you about yourself and your dreams?
- Is your present line of work (or course of studies, if you are a student) truly rewarding and fulfilling, at the spiritual level?
- If not, can you identify what you would rather be doing with your life? What *changes* are you willing to make to begin moving in that direction, and what might represent a manageable starting point?
- Projecting yourself many years into the future, what sort of *legacy* do you want to leave behind when you are finally ready to depart from this life?

Seek Guidance Along the Way

Our journey toward fulfilling our destiny is an exquisite dance: we alternate between retreating into the depths of our being to search for answers from our heart and venturing outward to do the legwork. Along the way, we seek counsel from others who have been placed in our path by providence to help us.

An appropriate analogy may be drawn to the recovery process. While we can diligently study the steps and spend hours poring over program literature, we inevitably reach a point where we need a trusted guide or sponsor to help us learn how to do the legwork in applying the program to our lives.

Likewise, in your spiritual quest to uncover your destiny and find the courage to follow your dreams, it is often helpful to augment your internal soul-searching with some structured growth work and exploration under the counsel of a trusted guide, confidant and teacher. As the saying goes, the teacher appears when the student is ready. The teacher you may be seeking at this point in your journey can appear in an infinite variety of forms. For example, you may choose to do some values clarification and growth work with a therapist or coach, a minister, priest, rabbi or other spiritual advisor, a teacher or mentor whom you truly look up to, your partner, a trusted friend—or any combination of the above.

Some of my own mentors have included psychotherapists, teachers who have left their mark, leaders in the wellness movement with whom I had the privilege of working, my loving wife, Ann, numerous bosses and coworkers, and even my pets! My foremost mentors in the field of wellness and recovery include a recovering alcoholic who served as a guest lecturer for a course in substance abuse I taught at a local college at an early point in my career and a close relative who modeled for me the qualities of courage and acceptance as he worked his 12-step program while struggling with a terminal illness. I also include among my mentors Dr. Andrew Weil, Deepak Chopra, Dean Ornish, the Dalai Lama and many other authors who have profoundly influenced my life through the inspirational teachings embodied in their writings.

Follow Your Dreams

Above all else, I urge you to create a life that is truly worth living by uncovering—and honoring—your dreams. One of my favorite quotes is the following statement, attributed to David Copperfield:

> *Whenever I pursue my dreams I discover something astonishing—I discover myself. My secret has been to consider nothing impossible. Then to treat possibilities as probabilities.*
>
> *I have learned that there are two ways I can live my life: following my dreams or doing something else. Dreams aren't a matter of chance but a matter of choice. When I dream, I believe that I am rehearsing my future.*

In following the pathway of the heart, it behooves us to listen to the messages that our dreams are attempting to reveal to us—whether these messages come to us while we are sleeping or in the form of daydreams. I had a profound experience several summers back while vacationing in the Sierras that vividly illustrates this point.

> *As I was hiking out from the little mountain village onto a new trail, winding high above the lakes toward the mountain peaks, I experienced a very vivid "waking dream." Climbing the trail, I fantasized that I was walking into a fog. As I continued on my journey, I was carried back through time to an early part of my childhood, to the little village in the Mohawk Valley of upstate New York where my father was born and raised.*
>
> *As I walked into the village, my younger self—"little Johnny"—appeared before me, carrying a candle. Appearing very*

confident and determined as he approached me through the foggy streets, he looked at me with a loving glance and handed me the candle. He smiled and said to me, "Here, take this candle and always let it burn brightly. Let it guide you through the foggy moments of despair that life may bring you. Let it serve as a guiding light, always beckoning you to keep your dreams in sight. Always follow your dreams!"

Shortly after returning from this vacation, I was inspired to begin writing this book. Needless to say, this particular "waking dream" imprinted in my heart a message that continues to influence me profoundly.

Do the Legwork

Once you have identified your calling or destiny, you need to get busy doing the legwork to transform your dreams into reality. Chances are, you are probably experiencing a significant gap between what you would like to be doing with your life and how you are living your day-to-day life. At this point, the important thing is to ask yourself, "How can I begin to close this gap, taking one step at a time?"

Be creative! Plot your goals, visualize a pathway leading to their realization, and identify some simple and manageable starting points. For example, if you would like to make a career shift, you most likely will need to come up with a pragmatic strategy for supporting yourself and your family while you are working through this transition.

Some simple and manageable starting points might include signing up for a course to get you headed in the right direction and researching alternative options for fulfilling whatever educational requirements you may need (including the growing number of universities with flexible programming that allows you to complete a significant portion of your studies online). Additionally, you will need to do some brainstorming with your spouse, partner or other significant people in your life who may help you identify creative options that will move you toward your chosen destiny. You may want to consider, for example, various ways of "lightening your load" on the material side to enable you to focus your energy on following your dreams. For example, do you really need that new car, or will "old faithful" (already paid for) carry you for another couple of years?

For the sake of illustration, I'll share with you some highlights from my own transformational journey.

In my late forties, while vacationing in the Sierras (again), I came to the realization that I wanted to become a psychotherapist. Having two mortgages on our house, I was in no position to simply quit my job and go back to school full-time. I was working in an area of health care in which job security was virtually nonexistent. I had to patiently bide my time while creating a reasonably secure base of employment that enabled me to focus my energies on completing my studies part-time. Finding a program that met my needs was a major challenge, since my full-time job as marketing director for a large medical group carried with it a daily, two-hour, round-trip commute. I tried out several programs before finding the right fit.

Finally, I located an innovative doctoral program based on a guided independent study model, which fulfilled the educational requirements for licensure as a psychologist in California. This program was a blessing, as it enabled me to complete my studies at my own pace and preserve some degree of balance in terms of quality of life with my family. After four and a half years of part-time studies, which I pursued as a hobby, I received my Ph.D. degree. In the process of completing my studies, I was able to do some groundbreaking research investigating the role of a wellness-oriented lifestyle in promoting successful recovery from chemical dependency.

After completing my studies, I found that the mental health field had tightened up considerably over the past decade, due to the influence of managed care. Searching for a creative way to carve a niche for myself, I hit upon the idea of writing this book.

I share these slices from my own journey in the hope that they may provide some helpful clues for embarking on your own transformational process. Over the course of my journey, I have found it particularly helpful to embrace the qualities of perseverance and flexibility. I'm talking about continuing to "chop wood and carry water" while pursuing my dreams—constantly holding my goal in sight, while keeping my eyes fixed on the terrain ahead of me and making the necessary course corrections along the way. Importantly, by viewing my doctoral studies as a hobby rather than as a burden, I was able to fully enjoy the journey.

Embracing Our Spirituality

To fully embrace the spiritual side of our nature, we need to attune ourselves to the many opportunities that life is constantly presenting to us. It is particularly important to give thanks for our blessings and release our resentments on a daily basis. Our lives are like the proverbial glass of water, we can view them as half empty or half full—it all boils down to what we choose to focus our awareness on. It is much more productive to count our blessings and focus on the many things that are working in our lives, rather than bemoan those areas in which we feel we may be lacking. This applies to matters relating to our physical health, as well as to our relationships, our careers and every other important aspect of our lives.

It is especially important to learn how to release our anger and practice the art of forgiveness. Clinging to resentment is akin to harboring a toxin in our bodies. In fact, unreleased resentment lies at the root of a wide range of physical ills. The act of forgiveness does not necessarily mean that we condone the action that hurt us. Through forgiveness, we are simply releasing our resentment toward the person or persons whom we feel have wronged us. In doing so, we free our energies to focus on the many blessings in our lives. Of course, in any relationship it is healthy to fight occasionally in order to clear the air. However, we should never go to bed at night harboring anger toward another, whether it is a spouse, child, friend or coworker. In his interpretive discourse on the Lord's Prayer, Emmett Fox recommends that every day we should make it a point to consciously forgive everyone whom we feel may have wronged us that day.

It is also important that we cultivate the art of taking miniature spiritual retreats throughout the day and weaving these retreats into our cycle of activities throughout the week. I'm talking about simple yet important sources of renewal, such as taking a few moments to enjoy a sunrise or sunset, occasionally driving to work along a slower, more scenic route, and creating the space in our lives to enjoy our evening meal as a time for communing with our loved ones. Taking time to appreciate nature can be especially renewing. As I previously mentioned, on weekends I love to drive away from the city and go hiking in the desert or the mountains. Our hobbies are also important sources of renewal, as they bring us closer to our spiritual core. It is critically important that we create the time to pursue these creative outlets in the midst of our hectic lives.

In summary, learning to cultivate and appreciate the spiritual side of our nature is a lifelong process and a critically important part of ensuring that we fully enjoy our journey.

As I am attempting to demonstrate throughout this book, pursuing a wellness lifestyle is a life-affirming process. In this chapter, we have focused on the importance of embracing your central purpose, nurturing your spirituality and creating a life worth living. The next chapter, fittingly, provides practical pointers for maximizing your prospects for living a long and healthy life. It addresses head-on the challenges posed by a major co-addiction that robs millions of recovering people of decades of joyful living.

10

Conquering Nicotine Addiction

This chapter addresses the devastating consequences that nicotine addiction has wrought on millions of people in recovery. If you are one of the millions of recovering alcoholics/addicts who are still smoking cigarettes, this chapter will provide you with very practical tips for freeing yourself from the grip of this deadly addiction. During my years of working in the addictions field, I have buried far too many friends and colleagues who worked their programs and abstained from their primary drugs of choice, only to succumb to the deadly consequences of cigarette smoking.

As you may be aware, cigarette smoking is the leading cause of preventable illness and death in the United States today. The role of smoking as a major contributing factor to cancer, heart disease, emphysema, osteoporosis and numerous other diseases is well established. Cigarette smoking causes approximately 440,000 deaths each year in the United States alone. Up to 65,000 nonsmokers die annually from the consequences of excessive exposure to secondhand smoke. On the average, male smokers cut their lives short by 13.2 years, and female smokers lose 14.5 years. As we will discuss shortly, people in recovery have an unusually high risk of succumbing to the hazards of tobacco use.

As a substance, cigarette smoke is a complex mixture of organic and inorganic compounds generated by the combustion of tobacco and various additives. The tar in cigarette smoke contains over 4,000 chemicals, including forty-three known carcinogens. Conservative estimates indicate that tobacco use causes one-third of all cancer deaths. Smoking is the direct cause of over 80 percent of all lung cancers and a major cause in cancers of the mouth, larynx, esophagus, kidney, bladder, pancreas and cervix. In addition, smoking triples the risk of dying from heart disease among middle-aged men and women, and smokers increase their risk of dying from bronchitis and emphysema by more than ten times. Smoking during pregnancy is associated with increased risk of preterm delivery and pregnancy complications.

Incidentally, if you are currently smoking or smoked for a number of years before quitting—or if you have suffered from prolonged, excessive exposure to secondhand smoke—you may wish to avail yourself of a recent advance in imaging technology called electron beam tomography (EBT). EBT, which enables radiologists to detect lung cancer in its early stages, when the disease is most treatable, is now available at leading medical centers across the country. (For more details, see the sidebar "This Test Can Save Your Life.")

This Test Can Save Your Life

Lung cancer is the most common cause of cancer deaths among both men and women in the United States, far eclipsing both prostate cancer in men and breast cancer in women. As a group, men and women with a history of alcoholism are at greater risk of lung cancer, due to the fact that the vast majority of alcoholics are heavy smokers—and many alcoholics continue to smoke after they have quit drinking.

Unfortunately, five out of six patients (83 percent) diagnosed with lung cancer will not survive five years. This is because chest X rays, the most commonly employed screening method, are generally not effective in early detection. By the time a cancer shows up on a chest X ray, the cancer has grown to the size of a quarter and may have already begun to spread throughout the body.

Fortunately, many imaging centers now offer lung scans employing new, state-of-the-art electron beam tomography (EBT) technology, which can detect lung cancer at an early stage. These scans produce highly definitive images that are able to detect lung cancer when the tumor is only the size of a grain of rice. Early detection dramatically increases prospects for long-term survival because it enables surgical intervention at the earlier stages of the disease. When lung cancer is discovered early (Stage 1), the disease is generally curable, with a long-term survival rate of over 85 percent.

Key at-risk groups for lung cancer are current smokers and ex-smokers—especially women, due to the significantly higher incidence of lung cancer among female smokers. Other groups at elevated risk for lung cancer include people in occupations involving major exposure to asbestos (for example, construction or shipyard workers and some auto mechanics), together with people who have been subjected to excessive, long-term exposure to second-hand smoke. This latter group includes many bartenders and servers, as well as family members of heavy smokers.

Lung scans employing the new EBT imaging technology are now available at growing numbers of imaging centers throughout the world. While most insurance plans do not currently cover this preventative procedure, it can represent a sound investment in your personal health enhancement strategy—particularly if you are currently smoking, are a former heavy smoker or if you fall into one of the other high-risk groups. To locate an EBT scanning facility in your area, either contact the imaging departments of major medical centers in your area or visit the GE Imatron Web site—*www.geimatron.com*—and click on "Find EBT locations."

Tip: Mention this book when you schedule your appointment, and ask if they can offer you a courtesy discount.

Smoking is also a major risk factor for heart disease, our nation's leading cause of death. The risk of developing heart disease for a pack-a-day smoker is double that for nonsmokers, with the risk rising directly in proportion to the amount of tobacco consumed.

Alcoholics and addicts, including those in recovery, are at particularly high risk for the many adverse health consequences associated with smoking. While the rate of tobacco use continues to decline among the general population, with less than one-fourth of all adults currently smoking, it is estimated that close to 90 percent of alcoholics continue to smoke. Sadly, a disproportionately high number of recovering alcoholics and addicts also continue to smoke, despite the fact that the majority would like to quit.

Alcoholism and Nicotine Dependency as Co-Addictions

A growing body of evidence suggests that alcoholism and nicotine dependency are co-addictions—that is, both addictions seem to go hand in hand. A nationwide survey of smoking behavior among both alcoholic and nonalcoholic subjects concluded that the relative risk of alcoholism is close to ten times greater for smokers than for nonsmokers. Significantly, this research involved a sample of several thousand subjects.

The National Institute on Alcohol Abuse and Alcoholism reports that between 80 and 95 percent of alcoholics smoke cigarettes, and that approximately 70 percent of alcoholics are heavy smokers, smoking more than one pack of cigarettes per day. Altogether, practicing alcoholics comprise approximately one-third of all smokers.

Various theories attempt to explain why so many alcoholics are also addicted to tobacco. As nicotine is a stimulant and alcohol is a depressant, it has been suggested that many alcoholics smoke heavily in part to counter the depressant effects associated with excessive drinking. Additionally, both nicotine and alcohol trigger the release of similar chemicals to the brain, contributing to habitual use of both substances. Chronic use of alcohol and nicotine also contributes to cross-tolerance—that is, decreased sensitivity to the effects of both substances. Cross-tolerance, in turn, leads to increased consumption of both alcohol and tobacco to obtain the sought after effects.

In terms of health consequences, numerous studies attest to the fact that the adverse effects of alcohol and tobacco compound each other to produce a heightened risk of illness and death associated with a host of conditions, including heart disease, lung cancer and other forms of cancer. According to the National Institute on Alcohol Abuse and Alcoholism, when compared to people who are both nonsmokers and nondrinkers, the relative risks of developing oral cancer are seven times greater for those who use tobacco alone, six times greater for those who use alcohol alone, and thirty-eight times greater for those who use both tobacco and alcohol.

If you are in the process of recovery from alcohol or drug addiction, you have no doubt witnessed firsthand the tragic toll that nicotine addiction takes on the recovery community.

In the late 1980s, I was hired by a psychiatric chain to develop a dual diagnosis chemical dependency program at one of their newer facilities. In the process of interviewing candidates for the senior counselor's position, I was expounding on my vision of implementing a program that would embody the principles of high-level wellness. One candidate was a female recovering alcoholic and a very seasoned counselor. She was also a chain smoker, who proceeded to chide me regarding my enthusiasm for wellness and recovery. She said, "You need to be careful not to take this too far." A year and a half later she was in the hospital, dying from lung cancer. A mutual friend, who was also a seasoned counselor, related that this woman had a habit of proudly proclaiming, "No one is ever going to make me stop smoking!" Unfortunately, she paid a very dear price for her nicotine addiction.

More recently, I had the sad experience of burying my brother-in-law, a recovering alcoholic with over a decade of sobriety under his belt. While he was drinking, he was also a heavy smoker. To make matters worse, he was an auto mechanic who suffered from asbestosis. He had been exposed excessively to asbestos while working on brakes for many years. Despite the fact that he had been free from both alcohol and tobacco for a number of years, his cumulative exposure to both substances eventually took its toll and he succumbed to lung cancer. By the time his health plan discovered the cancer, the tumor was inoperable.

The moral of both stories is that none of us is invincible. If you are one of the millions of recovering alcoholics and addicts who are still using tobacco, I urge you to make a firm commitment to kick this deadly habit. Later in this chapter we will present specific guidelines for freeing yourself from nicotine addiction. First, however, we need to debunk some of the more prevalent myths associated with smoking and recovery.

Myths Surrounding Smoking and Recovery

Historically, many people working in the addictions field have held some very erroneous assumptions regarding cigarette smoking and recovery. Some of the more prevalent myths include the following.

Myth Number One Cigarette smoking is a minor addiction that pales in comparison to the deadly consequences of the addict's drug of choice. Statistically, tobacco is by far the deadliest of drugs. According to the U.S. Department of Health and Human Services, some 440,000 Americans die annually from causes directly attributable to cigarette smoking. By comparison, alcohol abuse accounts for an estimated 125,000 to 150,000 deaths each year, heroin accounts for an estimated 4,000 deaths and cocaine accounts for an estimated 2,000 to 4,000 deaths.

Without intending to minimize the tragic consequences

associated with abuse of alcohol and illicit drugs, nicotine is clearly the most dangerous of all drugs in terms of its association with preventable death and disease. The argument among some treatment professionals that cigarette smoking is a comparatively "minor" addiction boils down to a rationalization that serves to justify their own smoking behavior.

Myth Number Two   **Attempting to quit smoking can sabotage your recovery from your primary addiction.** Unquestionably, nicotine is a highly addictive substance whose grip can be very difficult to overcome. I know this from personal experience, as I am a former smoker who has been clean from nicotine for over thirty years. I know what it's like to climb the walls when you're desperately trying to quit.

Despite nicotine's highly addictive properties, a growing body of evidence challenges the conventional wisdom of some treatment professionals who argue that attempting to quit smoking is tantamount to jeopardizing one's sobriety. In fact, some studies suggest that heavy smoking may be associated with an increased risk of relapse to drinking and drug use.

A San Francisco–based study focused on a sample of seventy-three recovering alcoholics with a history of heavy smoking, including a sub-sample of subjects who had successfully quit smoking. Significantly, none of the former smokers reported that their efforts to quit interfered with their ability to abstain from drinking. More recently, a study based at the University of Vermont focused on 115 heavy smokers with a history of alcoholism. Study subjects were randomly given either a nicotine patch or a placebo. Significantly, the researchers found that none of the participants experienced either drinking problems or increases in alcohol craving.

In another study focusing on alcoholics undergoing treatment, researchers discovered that the more dependent drinkers also tended to be heavy smokers. Investigators observed that both nicotine and alcohol appear to trigger similar internal chemical responses as part of a general coping mechanism. They then speculated that heavy smokers may be at greater risk of returning to drinking when they are under heavy stress because of increased urge to drink triggered by their nicotine dependency.

While freeing yourself from nicotine addiction can be challenging, there is no convincing evidence that attempting to quit will undermine your ability to abstain from your primary drug(s) of choice. In fact, accumulating evidence suggests that successfully quitting smoking may actually contribute to reduced risk of relapse.

Myth Number Three Most recovering alcoholics/addicts don't really want to stop smoking. This is yet another myth that fails to stand up to scrutiny. A study of alcoholics/addicts completing inpatient treatment at a VA hospital documented that the greater majority (80 percent) were daily smokers. Among the smoking subjects, 42 percent expressed an interest in stopping smoking at the time of treatment, while an additional 38 percent reported that they would like to quit smoking within a year of completing treatment.

My own research, focusing on a sample of fifty alcoholics and addicts who had completed residential treatment, yielded similar findings. While the greater majority of subjects in my study were smokers (82 percent), close to two-thirds of the smokers (66 percent) reported that they planned to quit smoking within the next two years—indicating a strong desire to kick the habit.

Available evidence suggests that the greater majority of recovering alcoholics and addicts who are currently smoking would really like to quit. If you fall into this category, don't despair. The next section presents specific guidelines to assist you in successfully conquering your nicotine addiction.

Guidelines for Successfully Kicking the Habit

Due to the highly addictive nature of nicotine and your prior chemical dependency history, you stand to benefit from a strategic approach to smoking cessation that is custom-tailored to the special needs of recovering alcoholics and addicts. The following guidelines can help you successfully quit smoking and add many healthy years to your life. Follow these suggestions to develop and implement your own strategic plan for quitting.

Set a Quit Date

If you are ready to "bite the bullet," set a target quit date for sometime in the next thirty days and notify your friends, family and coworkers of your intentions.

If you are not yet ready to commit to a quit date, make a note to revisit this important issue when you conduct your quarterly wellness inventory (more about this in chapter 12). If you are serious about quitting smoking, you need to be willing to make a firm commitment to quit within the next twelve to eighteen months—hopefully sooner!

Use a Holistic Stop-Smoking Strategy

I purposely placed this chapter here, *following* the chapters about the core dimensions of wellness, because I really want you to have a "full toolbox" at your disposal to combat this deadly addiction! You can now incorporate the benefits of exercise, stress management, sound nutrition and a strong social support system into a holistic strategy that will help you quit smoking for good. Regular aerobic exercise, effective stress management and other components of a wellness-oriented lifestyle all interact synergistically to help you get through those difficult first thirty days.

This integrated, lifestyle-oriented approach to quitting is the foundation of the sound and effective strategies for smoking cessation recommended by the American Cancer Society (ACS), American Lung Association (ALA) and other organizations dedicated to combating nicotine addiction. For specific pointers regarding dietary modifications that can help curb your dependency on nicotine, see the sidebar "Diet and Nicotine Withdrawal" on page 167.

See Your Primary Care Physician for Help and Information

Coordinate your plans to quit smoking with your primary care physician. As doctors are intimately familiar with the adverse consequences of nicotine addiction, your doctor should fully support your plans to quit. If you are a heavy smoker who has been "hooked" for a number of years, you may want to discuss with your doctor the pros and cons of incorporating nicotine replacement therapy or Zyban into your smoking cessation program. **Caution:** Only use nicotine replacement therapies under medical supervision. This is especially true for anyone with a history of chemical dependency.

Develop a Strong Support System

As part of your stop-smoking strategy, it's important to develop a strong social support system that supports your quitting smoking for good. Along these lines, I highly recommend:

- Eliciting the support of friends, family and coworkers—especially nonsmokers.
- Taking advantage of one of the low-cost group support programs offered by the ACS, ALA and other community agencies. Both ACS and ALA offer low-cost, professionally facilitated stop-smoking programs employing a group support model. Also check and see what your health plan has to offer. These programs are highly effective and have helped millions of people successfully kick the habit.
- Calling one of the many toll-free "quit lines" for smokers. Check with directory assistance or your state's health department for the help-line telephone number serving your community.

Use Your 12-Step Program for Support

Fully use your 12-step program to help you quit smoking. If you are working a 12-step program for your primary addiction, it is probably a good idea to double up on meetings during your first thirty days as a new nonsmoker. Be sure to attend nonsmoking meetings!

You may also want to consider the following pointers for effectively using 12-step resources in helping you over the hump:

- Elicit your sponsor's help in staying off cigarettes, if he or she is a nonsmoker. If your primary sponsor is still smoking, you may wish to link up with a secondary sponsor who is a nonsmoking, recovering alcoholic/addict.
- Consider attending Nicotine Anonymous meetings, in addition to maintaining regular attendance at your home group meetings. The nationwide toll-free number for Nicotine Anonymous is 800-642-0666.

Practice Positive Visualization

Each night before drifting off to sleep, spend a couple of minutes visualizing yourself enjoying a lifetime of freedom from smoking. See yourself watching your children and grandchildren growing up, and visualize yourself accomplishing the dreams that are closest to your heart.

Diet and Nicotine Withdrawal

If you are serious about quitting smoking, you should pay particular attention to the role of diet and exercise in your overall strategy for kicking the habit. The following dietary pointers can go a long way toward helping you over the hump of nicotine withdrawal.

When you are quitting smoking, be sure to start the day with a nutritious breakfast—preferably a breakfast rich in complex carbohydrates, such as whole grain cereal or oatmeal and fruit. While many smokers tend to skip breakfast, this can easily sabotage your efforts to quit by triggering a midmorning dip in blood sugar that heightens nicotine cravings.

Foods rich in complex carbohydrates—including fresh vegetables and fruits, and whole grain breads and pasta—are important dietary mainstays for anyone who is quitting smoking. These foods help the body produce adequate supplies of serotonin, a biochemical that interacts with the brain to serve as a natural mood elevator. Serotonin helps counteract the momentary bouts of depression that may accompany nicotine withdrawal.

Whole-food sources of protein, including beans, soy products, fish and poultry, also play a role in combating nicotine withdrawal. In addition to contributing to production of serotonin, protein-rich foods are helpful in maintaining alertness throughout the day.

A Note About Weight Gain: Weight gain is a top concern among ex-smokers. Don't be surprised if you temporarily gain between two and five pounds during your first months of freedom from tobacco. Nicotine is an appetite suppressant, and it tends to raise the metabolic rate slightly. Hence, some modest weight gain may be a part of the body's overall adjustment process. You can minimize this tendency to gain weight by consciously choosing nutrient-dense, low-calorie foods while quitting smoking and by snacking on raw vegetables, fruits, rice cakes and other low-calorie items.

Be sure to increase your involvement in physical exercise as you go through nicotine withdrawal. Not only will exercise naturally energize you—helping to hold your cravings for nicotine at bay—it will also help you maintain a normal weight level during the withdrawal process. If you do put on a few extra pounds while quitting, you should generally be able to return easily to your normal weight level within a few months by making sensible food choices and increasing your energy expenditure.

How to Handle Withdrawal

Once you have made a firm commitment to your quit date and have formulated your strategy for quitting, you will need to navigate the nicotine withdrawal process. The following tips should help you over this hurdle:

- Before you quit, write down your main reason for quitting on a card—and always carry this card with you. Over the weeks and months ahead, constantly refer to this card whenever you are tempted to smoke.
- Have your last cigarette the night before your quit day then throw away all cigarettes and matches.
- Remind yourself that nicotine withdrawal symptoms are temporary, generally lasting ten to fourteen days before noticeably subsiding. Remember to take the first week or two of withdrawal "one day at a time."
- The key to successfully handling withdrawal is incorporating "substitute activities" for smoking into your lifestyle. Be

creative. Try chewing gum rather than smoking, snacking on fruits and raw vegetables, and walking or running when you get the urge for a cigarette.

- Learn to "reframe" your withdrawal symptoms. Interpret these symptoms as positive signs that you are cleansing your body from nicotine. Visualize yourself as a nonsmoker who is beginning to enjoy being free from nicotine for the rest of your life.

- Remember to avoid (when possible) "people, places and things" that may trigger the urge to smoke. Being around people who are smoking during your first two weeks of withdrawal can be especially stressful. If you used to hang out with your "smoking buddies" during breaks at work, you now need to surround yourself with nonsmoking friends. Make a special point of attending nonsmoking 12-step meetings, and announce to the group that you just quit smoking. Be creative—ask for a hug when you are tempted to "light up."

- Politely yet assertively request that your smoking friends refrain from smoking when they are with you. When you find yourself in the company of people who are smoking, practice reframing. Rather than envying them for smoking, remind yourself that you are grateful that you are no longer polluting your body with tobacco and its many toxic ingredients.

Reprogramming Your Smoking Triggers

Just as you have learned to reprogram your "trigger points" in overcoming your primary addiction to alcohol and/or other drugs, you must likewise consciously reprogram those triggers that you associate with "lighting up." Common triggers associated with smoking include:

- Working under pressure
- Feeling blue
- Drinking coffee or other caffeinated beverages
- Being around people who are smoking
- Feeling the need to take a break from work
- Any pleasurable activity that you habitually associate with smoking (for example, enjoying a cigarette after dinner)

The key to effectively coping with triggers is *planning ahead.* After you identify the key triggers associated with your smoking behavior, consciously substitute an alternative response. For example:

- Instead of lighting up a cigarette when you feel blue, go outside and run around the block (exercise is a good antidote for "the blues").
- Instead of taking a cigarette break during work, drink a glass of fruit juice or spend a few minutes socializing with a non-smoking coworker.
- Instead of smoking after dinner, take a walk or listen to some favorite music.

It is also important to *avoid* your triggers whenever possible, especially during the first two weeks of withdrawal. For example, if you normally smoke when you're drinking coffee, try drinking herbal tea. Likewise, if you associate smoking with watching TV, read a book instead. Whenever the urge to smoke is especially strong, take out your card and review your primary reason for quitting smoking.

Slips and Relapses

Due to the highly addictive nature of nicotine, slips and relapses are common. When slips occur, you need to immediately get back on course and avoid getting discouraged. Again, practice the principle of "one day at a time."

A slip is a momentary setback where you have one or two cigarettes. As you are quitting smoking, be sure to remind yourself that a slip is not a relapse (a return to habitual smoking). If you experience a slip, remind yourself that you are a nonsmoker who has had a *momentary setback*. Don't be too hard on yourself—allow yourself to be human. Then get back on track with your new program as a "habitual nonsmoker."

A slip can be a valuable teacher, and you need to ask yourself, "What can I learn from this?" Discuss your slip with your non-smoking sponsor and elicit his or her guidance on avoiding future lapses. It is vital to reflect on what triggered the slip and how you can effectively cope with similar situations in the future without "lighting up."

Even if you suffer a relapse and return to habitual smoking, don't get discouraged. Be persistent! Most smokers quit smoking several times before they finally quit for good. Rather than beating yourself up, simply redouble your determination to get back on track to a smoke-free lifestyle. As is the case with all aspects of recovery, you need to focus on your successes, learn from your failures and then let them go. Set a new quit date (this should be sometime in the next thirty to sixty days), and rally your support system.

More Strategies for Quitting Smoking

At the beginning of this section, I emphasized the importance of developing your own customized strategy for quitting smoking. Over and beyond these suggestions, you may also wish to consider incorporating some additional strategies.

Traditional and Alternative Therapeutic Approaches

Many former smokers have used a variety of therapeutic approaches to help them through the early days of nicotine withdrawal. We've already mentioned the possible benefits of nicotine replacement therapy in easing the withdrawal process for heavy smokers. If you choose to use nicotine replacement therapy, you need to be on guard against lapsing into addiction to the nicotine replacement itself. This is an important reason why nicotine replacement therapy should only be used under strict medical supervision.

Other former smokers have used alternative therapies, including acupuncture and massage, to help them kick the habit. If either of these methods appeals to you, I'd encourage you to try it.

You might also consider incorporating clinical hypnosis into your smoking cessation program—especially if you have unsuccessfully tried to quit smoking on several occasions. In the hands of a skilled professional, hypnosis takes you into a state of heightened suggestibility. Then, your subconscious mind is "programmed" to lend its full support to *whatever* changes you are attempting to make. I am convinced that clinical hypnosis is an extremely powerful vehicle for facilitating the mind-body healing connection at many levels. If you are interested in incorporating hypnosis into your program, you can either purchase a smoking cessation tape or schedule a session with a professional hypnotherapist. This should be a practitioner with specific expertise in smoking cessation, preferably someone who is attuned to the special circumstances of recovering alcoholics and addicts.

Get Additional Support Online

The Internet contains a wealth of sites targeted to people who are trying to quit smoking. In particular, you may want to check out the Web sites sponsored by the American Cancer Society, American Lung Association and American Heart Association. One of my own favorite health-related Web sites is *www.Helios Health.com*, which hosts an extensive page of well thought-out instructive materials for quitting smoking.

Reward Yourself!

In attempting to reprogram any ingrained behavior, it is critically important to reward yourself at important milestones. For example, treat yourself and your partner to a special dinner at the end of your first week as a nonsmoker, and plan a celebration once you reach the thirty-day mark. You may also want to plan a weekend out of town or a special vacation at some point down the road. If you're a pack-a-day smoker, you are currently spending over four dollars a day to support your habit. Use some of the money you will be saving to reward yourself for quitting!

In conclusion, if you are one of the millions of recovering alcoholics and addicts who are still smoking, you owe it to yourself and your loved ones to make a firm commitment to quit. This is by far the greatest single step that you can take to add years of healthful living to your life expectancy and dramatically improve your quality of life. If you are one of the fortunate ones who has already quit smoking (or who never started), please be sure to share this chapter with your friends and loved ones who are still suffering from nicotine addiction.

As I advocate a holistic approach to integrating a wellness-oriented lifestyle into your recovery program, I urge you to follow your own customized smoking cessation program within the context of your wellness plan.

Let's now move on to part three of this book, which presents detailed guidelines for developing your personal blueprint for optimal health.

Your Personal Blueprint for Wellness and Recovery

11

Conducting Your Personal
Wellness Assessment

The preceding chapters have focused on teaching you the various dimensions of wellness and inspiring you to apply these principles in your daily life. This chapter is designed to place you in the driver's seat by guiding you through a wellness assessment process, customized to your unique circumstances. By actively participating in the exercises that follow, you will take charge of your health and begin reaping the many benefits associated with a wellness lifestyle.

The Wellness Assessment Process

Wellness Lifestyle Assessment Questionnaire

At the end of this chapter you will find a Wellness Lifestyle Assessment Questionnaire and Scoring Guide, followed by a

Vital Signs and Health Assessment Worksheet. When completed, these two forms will be the road map for the first leg of your journey to high-level wellness.

The assessment questionnaire is adapted from the survey I conducted for my doctoral dissertation, which focused on the association between a wellness-oriented lifestyle and successful sobriety maintenance. As previously discussed, study subjects were divided into two groups: the successful recovery group, who maintained sobriety following completion of primary treatment; and the relapse group, who subsequently relapsed to their former drinking/drugging.

In the version of the questionnaire used in my study, the highest possible score was 90 points. The higher the score, the healthier the subject's lifestyle. Significantly, the average score for subjects in the successful recovery group was 55, compared with an average score of 39 for subjects in the relapse group. As the likelihood of this difference occurring by chance is less than one in one thousand, these findings strongly suggest that a wellness lifestyle goes hand in hand with successful sobriety.

The version of the questionnaire used in this book has been expanded to include the important dimension of central purpose. With this addition, the highest possible score is 100 points. In addition, the questionnaire includes two unscored background items that address your degree of involvement in your 12-step or other recovery-focused program.

I invite you to take a few minutes to complete the Wellness Lifestyle Assessment Questionnaire beginning on page 197. Please answer each item as accurately as possible, choosing the one response for each question that most nearly reflects your present circumstances. Before you begin, you may wish to make several blank copies for future use. As you become more actively involved in pursuing optimal health, you will probably want to retake the questionnaire periodically to assess your progress. After you have completed the questionnaire, tally your score, referring to the scoring guide on pages 201–202.

Use Your Responses to Uncover Your Strengths and Weaknesses

Hopefully, your wellness index score and your responses to individual items will provide you with valuable clues concerning your current strong points and weak links in planning a wellness lifestyle.

In interpreting your overall score, remember that it is simply a baseline indicator of where you stand now. If you scored 75 or higher, this indicates that you are already doing many of the right things, and this book will reinforce what you are already doing and provide valuable suggestions for fine-tuning and raising the bar. If you scored below 75, you have some work ahead of you in charting a pathway to optimal health.

I encourage you to pay attention to whatever clues your responses to the individual items provide in terms of zeroing in on your long-range wellness goals, as well as your more immediate, action-oriented objectives. Pay particular attention to your responses to question 17, which asks you to rate your overall state of health, together with question 18, which focuses on how much control you believe you have over matters affecting your health. Regarding question 17, if you currently rate your state of health as "fair" or "poor," then I would challenge you to make those lifestyle changes that will help move your health status into the "reasonably good" range. Once you have reached that point, you may want to raise the bar and strive towards eventually placing yourself within the "excellent" category.

Likewise, how you respond to question 18—which assesses where you stand in relation to what social scientists call the health-related locus of control—speaks volumes about how much power you believe you have over matters affecting your health. Refer back to the chart in chapter 3 entitled "Factors Influencing a Person's Health" (page 30). You will recall that the majority of factors influencing your state of health—including lifestyle influences and behaviors, environmental influences, and your use of health care services—all represent areas of your life where you can exercise a substantial degree of control by virtue of the choices you make.

As you take a proactive stance in defining your wellness goals and executing your strategic plan for bringing these goals to fruition, you will see that you have a great degree of control over matters affecting your health. This perception will have a snow-balling effect, propelling you further along in your journey toward optimal health. Even if you are struggling with heart disease, cancer or another life-threatening illness, you will find that you are able to open up whole new vistas for dramatically improving both your overall health and quality of life by making a firm commitment to *take charge of your health*.

I would also encourage you to take note of your responses to the three 10-point items: namely, question 8, which deals with your level of commitment to a regular exercise program; question 11, which addresses nicotine addiction; and question 15, which focuses on the presence of a strong sense of central purpose in your life. If you scored a 10 in each of these key items, you are well along the way to reaping the benefits of high-level wellness. If you scored less than 10 on any of these items, I encourage you to reflect on the importance of these areas in your life when you complete the goal-setting and priorities exercises in the following chapter.

Important: Do not beat yourself up if your score falls short of where you would like it to be. As they say in AA, our objective here is progress, not perfection. Again, your initial score is simply a going-in, baseline score, which will assist you in customizing your program and moving toward optimal health and personal fulfillment.

Vital Signs and Health Assessment Worksheet

Let's move on to the second assessment form presented in this chapter, the Vital Signs and Health Assessment Worksheet beginning on page 203. Again, before completing this portion of your assessment, make several copies of the form for future use.

The first section of this worksheet, Basic Wellness Vital Signs, summarizes important indicators of your present health status, with particular reference to cardiovascular fitness. Consult your doctor's office to obtain the values for each item, as measured in your most recent physical examination. If you have not had a physical within the past two years, you should schedule an examination to get baseline measures of your current health status. Once you have obtained your current measures for each of the basic wellness vital signs, enter them in this section of your worksheet.

Let's take a few minutes to discuss the relevance of these vital signs.

Body Mass Index (BMI)

Your body weight in relation to your height (without shoes on) allows for computation of your body mass index (BMI), a *key indicator* of your overall health status.

To compute your BMI, visit the National Heart, Lung and Blood Institute Web site at *www.nhlbisupport.com/bmi*. Enter your current height and weight on the Body Mass Index page, and the program will calculate your BMI rating. Alternatively, you can compute your BMI yourself by multiplying your weight in pounds by 703, and dividing this figure by your height in inches squared.

According to guidelines issued by the National Institutes of Health, your BMI should be less than 25 in order to promote optimal health. A BMI of 25 or higher is considered overweight, and a BMI of 30 or higher is considered obese. Ironically, despite a high level of public knowledge in matters relating to health and fitness, recent nationwide studies indicate that close to two-thirds of adult Americans are either overweight or obese.

Your BMI is important because people who are overweight are more likely to develop elevated blood pressure and cholesterol levels, which are associated with increased risk of heart disease. By bringing your BMI within the desirable range, you are likely to reduce your risk of developing heart disease significantly— along with diabetes and other metabolic disorders, as well as many forms of cancer.

Blood Pressure

Our resting blood pressure is another important wellness vital sign. Elevated blood pressure places an extra burden on the heart, forcing it to work harder to pump blood throughout the body. It is important to know your blood pressure level, because high blood pressure, called hypertension, is associated with increased risk of heart disease and stroke.

Your blood pressure level consists of two readings—your systolic pressure, which is recorded when your heart is pumping, and your diastolic pressure, which reflects your blood pressure when your heart is at rest. As our blood pressure can vary considerably throughout the day, reflecting our varying mental, emotional and physiological stress levels, it may be necessary to take several readings to arrive at an accurate assessment.

According to guidelines issued by the National Heart, Lung and Blood Institute, normal blood pressure is defined as a systolic/diastolic reading of less than 120/80 (read as 120 over 80). A reading ranging from 120 to 139 systolic and 80 to 89 diastolic is considered "prehypertensive," and a reading ranging from 140 to 159 systolic and 90 to 99 diastolic is regarded as "stage one hypertension."

If your blood pressure level (after several readings) falls within the prehypertensive or hypertensive ranges, you should obtain medical guidance to help you reduce your blood pressure. More likely than not, the recommendations presented in this book concerning diet, exercise and stress management will be of considerable help.

Resting Heart Rate

As the name implies, this is your heart rate when your heart is at rest. The best time to test your resting heart rate is in the morning, after a good night's sleep. Take your pulse for fifteen seconds and multiply that number by four.

A resting heart rate ranging from 60 to 72 beats per minute is considered normal, and a rate below 60 is considered very good. As is the case with blood pressure, as a general rule the lower your resting heart rate, the better. Resting heart rates tend to be lower among people in good physical condition, as the heart does not need to work as hard to pump blood through the body. Some athletes in top condition have resting heart rates in the fifties and, occasionally, even in the forties.

Cholesterol Level

Serum cholesterol level is a well-documented risk factor associated with heart disease and stroke. Our risk of heart disease increases significantly as our cholesterol level rises. If you don't know your current cholesterol level, ask your physician to order this simple and inexpensive test for you.

In accordance with American Heart Association guidelines, a blood cholesterol level of less than 200 is desirable, a level ranging from 200 to 239 is borderline high, and a level of 240 or above is definitely considered high blood cholesterol. Statistically, a person with a cholesterol level of 240 or higher has twice the risk of heart disease as a person with a reading of less than 200.

Some eighty million Americans have elevated cholesterol levels, defined as a cholesterol reading of 200 or above. The extremely high incidence of elevated cholesterol among the American public is largely attributable to the typical American diet, which by worldwide standards is extremely high in saturated fat. Cholesterol levels approaching 200 are virtually unheard of in parts of the world where dietary staples consist predominantly of vegetables, fruits and whole-grain sources of protein, with minimal consumption of animal products.

From a health improvement perspective, I encourage you to attain a cholesterol reading that is significantly below the 200 level that is considered normal by conventional medical standards. This recommendation is borne out by the Framingham Heart Study, an ongoing federally sponsored study initiated in 1948 that continues to shed light on the role of various risk factors in heart disease. Significantly, Dr. William Castelli, the study's medical director, reports that no one in the study with a cholesterol level of less than 150 has ever had a heart attack.

What are the ramifications of high cholesterol levels for personal wellness planning? As a rule, if your current cholesterol level is above 200, you should definitely work with your doctor to bring your cholesterol level down to a more acceptable range. In my opinion, transitioning to a whole foods–based diet that emphasizes nutrient-dense, plant-based food sources (as discussed in chapter 5) represents an important step in bringing down cholesterol levels. Also strive to get a better handle on managing stress, as our bodies manufacture more cholesterol when we are under excessive stress.

In terms of achieving optimal health, I would encourage you to *eventually* strive for a cholesterol level of 180 or lower—or, even better, the level of 160 or lower found in many athletes. Along these lines, the classic bestseller *Dr. Dean Ornish's Program for Reversing Heart Disease*, provides excellent guidelines concerning dietary measures designed to promote optimum cardiovascular health.

Let me emphasize that you should not be discouraged if your cholesterol level is currently above the desirable range.

Remember, wellness is a transitional process. The critically important first step is to identify where you are now so you can identify those corrective measures that you would like to initiate. If your cholesterol level is currently on the high side, consider this as a going-in baseline figure, and look forward to tracking the progressive reduction in your level over the months ahead as you proactively take charge of your health.

Other Significant Health-Related Indicators

The information that you record in this section is intended to round out your health status overview and assist you in formulating your wellness action plan. Enter any pertinent findings from relevant screening tests—mammograms, pap smears, and tests for colorectal cancer, prostate cancer, glaucoma, etc.—as well as any abnormal lab readings noted during your most recent physical exam. Also make note of any other significant indicators relating to your overall health status that are not covered by the basic vital signs.

Pinpointing Your Current Strengths and Weaknesses

Let's now move on to the part of your wellness assessment worksheet that focuses on pinpointing your current strengths and weaknesses in relation to your overall health status. This part of the assessment is divided into two sections—your personal health history and health-related behaviors, and your family health history.

Personal Health History and Health-Related Behaviors

Strong Points:

In this section, highlight your current strong points relating to your overall health status, together with those positive attitudes, attributes and health-related behaviors that will accelerate your journey to optimal health. Examples of items to highlight include:

- Your recovery track record. If you have successfully abstained from alcohol and drugs for several years, this is a *major strength* that indicates you possess the resiliency and adaptability to propel yourself along your personal journey to high-level wellness.
- Objective indicators of positive health status. Note those areas where your basic vital signs (such as blood pressure and cholesterol level) and other indicators are within the desirable range. Even if a particular reading falls outside of the desired range, if you are already making progress toward reversing this situation, that is a definite strong point that should be noted.
- Attitudes and behaviors. Are you ready to commit yourself to a wellness lifestyle, and are you willing to do the legwork? Have you already undertaken any positive changes in diet, exercise and other health-related behaviors since you started reading this book? These are all positive strengths that should be identified and celebrated.
- Social supports. Do you enjoy a strong social support system, through friends, family and other sources of support? This is another positive strength.

- Central purpose. Do you see yourself as a person with a strong sense of purpose in your life who translates your dreams into reality? If you are making progress along this journey, then you are well along the way to manifesting high-level wellness.

Weak Links:

Scanning our personal health histories, we all have our weak links, as well as areas of strength. One of my own weak links is a childhood history of seasonal allergies (hay fever), which has translated to a somewhat heightened susceptibility to colds and flu in my adult life.

We need to be aware of our weak links, as well as our strengths, so we can identify effective strategies for shoring up our areas of weakness. For example, my susceptibility to winter bouts of flu has served as a motivating factor for adopting a diet that places heavy emphasis on "live foods" in the form of fresh vegetables and fruits. My concern with strengthening my immune system has also motivated me to tone down my hectic schedule and attain a better balance between activity and rest. Likewise, I have learned to view my tendency to experience hyperacidity (excessive stomach acid) when under too much stress as a sign that I need to get a better handle on managing stressful situations in my life.

In highlighting your own health-related weak links, reflect on how these areas may serve as valuable motivators to help you make needed changes that will bring your life into better balance. Examples of items that are appropriate to highlight in the weak links section include:

- Any personal history of either acute or chronic illness, such as heart disease, hypertension, diabetes, asthma or cancer.
- Any vital sign readings, signs or symptoms that indicate desirable areas of improvement—for example, high blood pressure, elevated cholesterol, a tendency to experience excessive tension headaches or chronic muscular tension, excessive body weight, etc.
- Detrimental health-related behaviors that threaten to undermine your journey to optimal health—for example, cigarette smoking, excessive caffeine consumption, junk food addictions, etc.

Note that sometimes the presence of a serious health-related problem may be indicative of *both* strengths and weaknesses. For example, if you have suffered a heart attack in the past, your history of heart disease is definitely a weak link. By the same token, if your experience of surviving a heart attack has motivated you to make needed changes in your lifestyle in reference to diet, exercise and stress management—and has served as a wake-up call to reflect on what is truly important in your life—then these corresponding shifts in your attitudes and behaviors represent major strengths that should be noted and celebrated.

Family Health History

Strong Points:

Look at your family of origin, particularly your parents, and reflect on significant family influences that may have a bearing on both your current health status and your prospects of living to a healthy, ripe old age. Parental influences that can have a direct bearing on your health status include your genetic predispositions (such as a genetic trait toward alcoholism), as well as acquired health-related behavioral patterns that tend to run in your family.

In identifying the health-related strong points within your own family history, consider the following:

- Does longevity tend to run on either side of your family (or better still, on both sides)? Was either of your parents particularly long lived? A positive response to either question suggests that you may have inherited programming that can set the stage for a long and healthy life—if you don't mess with the program!

- Looking back over your family tree, does your family appear to be relatively free from either cancer or heart disease? If so, this is a good sign in terms of your biological programming.

- Can you identify any positive health-related attitudes or behaviors that have been passed down through your family? Using my wife's family as an example, Ann's parents were second-generation Americans of Italian and French descent who passed on a number of health-conducive traditions to their children. These include an emphasis on eating light on the food chain, together with a respect for herbs and other natural healing remedies. Ann reports that one of her father's favorite sayings was "I'll trust nature over science any day!" If you can identify similar positive health-related attitudes that are characteristic of your family, be sure to note and celebrate these strengths.

- Also reflect on any particularly positive attitudes regarding life in general that your parents may have passed along. In my case, I am thankful that both my parents modeled an appreciation for cultivating knowledge, together with a strong work ethic and an overriding sense of integrity. And my wife's mother, Louise, led a life that portrayed the classic embodiment of the Serenity Prayer.

Weak Links:

In focusing on the other side of your family's health history, attempt to identify any potential weak links that might be associated with the health histories of your parents and their forebears. For example:

- Are any particular patterns of illness, or causes of death, prevalent in your family tree? What are these, and what ramifications do they pose for you?
- What potential weak links are suggested by your parents' health histories? For example, did either of your parents die before age 65? If so, what was the cause of death, and did this parent perhaps contribute unwittingly to their early demise by clinging to unhealthy lifestyle or behavioral patterns? What ramifications does this pose concerning your own wellness lifestyle planning?

    Using my own family as an example, my father suffered from elevated blood pressure throughout most of his adult life and died from a heart attack at age sixty-one. While my dad was quite athletic in both high school and college, once he began his career as a teacher he adopted a very sedentary lifestyle. He was also overweight, was a pack-a-day smoker throughout most of his adult life and was not particularly adept at managing day-to-day stresses. On top of this, he was diagnosed with Type 2 diabetes in his late fifties—a condition that accelerates the progression of heart disease if left untreated.

From a wellness perspective, the sad experience of seeing my father cut down in his prime of life due to heart disease has motivated both me and my brothers to take extra precautions regarding known risk factors associated with heart disease. As preventative measures, I exercise daily, attempt to minimize my fat intake by following a semivegetarian diet, practice meditation twice a day as part of my personal stress management program, and constantly remind myself to slow down and smell the roses. I also pay particular attention to my vital signs relating to cardiovascular fitness (blood pressure, cholesterol level and resting heart rate) and take whatever steps I can to keep these within the desirable ranges.

• Also examine your family tree to determine whether any prominent negative attitudes or health-related behaviors stand out. Examples could include a fatalistic view concerning health, accompanied by a lack of focus in regard to taking care of oneself; a familial tendency to abuse alcohol and other substances (including tobacco); and unhealthy eating patterns accompanied by lack of exercise. If these, or other negative attitudes or behaviors are prevalent in your family of origin, what ramifications do they pose for you in terms of personal wellness planning?

Again, the purpose of pausing to assess the various weak links associated with our family health histories is not to "beat up on our parents." Rather, we should be concerned with identifying potential warning signs as we actively take charge of our health so we can maximize our prospects for living a long, healthy life and fulfilling our heartfelt dreams.

Setting Your Longevity Goal

In completing this section of your assessment, you need to do a bit of soul-searching, focusing on honest responses to the following questions:

- How long would you *ideally* like to live, if you could reach this age in a relatively robust state of health?
- Realistically, how long do you *expect* to live, if you make no changes in your present lifestyle?

While zeroing in on your desired life expectancy may seem like an academic exercise if you are in your twenties or thirties, please pause for a moment and do some serious reflecting on these seminal questions. Wouldn't you like to live long enough to enjoy seeing your grandchildren (and great-grandchildren) growing up? Don't you have some heartfelt dreams concerning your mission in life that you would like to nurture into fruition?

If you have been completely honest with yourself, you will probably see a significant gap between how long you would ideally like to live and how long you can realistically expect to live—assuming that you make no changes in your present lifestyle. This is where the real work begins. Focusing on the difference between these two numbers, ask yourself what steps immediately come to mind that you can take to begin to *bridge the gap*. Jot these thoughts down on your assessment sheet. They will provide valuable clues for developing your customized wellness and longevity plan.

Finally, take a moment to focus on some immediate health-related goals that you would like to accomplish concerning your current health status and quality of life. For example, would you like to see yourself enjoying increased energy and vitality? Would you like to get rid of that tire around your waistline? Note your immediate wellness goals on your assessment form. They will provide valuable grist for the mill as you move on to the action planning and implementation process outlined in the following chapter.

In this chapter, you have taken major strides toward taking charge of your health. You have conducted your baseline wellness assessment, identified your going-in longevity goal and started thinking about the steps you can take toward charting your pathway to optimal health. Let's now move on to chapter 12 and the action planning stage. Here you will crystallize both your long-term wellness goals and immediate short-range priorities, together with specific action-oriented steps that will transform these goals into reality. Read on!

Wellness Lifestyle
Assessment Questionnaire

Name: _____

Date: _____

Age: _____

Instructions: Answer each item as accurately as possible. Please check the *one response* for each question that most nearly reflects your present circumstances.

Background Items:

1. How long have you been working your recovery program?

   _____

2. How often do you currently attend 12-step meetings (or meetings of your chosen recovery-focused support group)?
   - ○ a. Daily
   - ○ b. Several times a week
   - ○ c. Once a week
   - ○ d. Less than once a week
   - ○ e. Do not currently attend meetings

Lifestyle Items:

3. I see a doctor for a general medical checkup at least once every two years:
   - ○ a. Yes
   - ○ b. No

4. I get at least seven to eight hours of sleep at night:
   - ○ a. Always
   - ○ b. Most of the time
   - ○ c. Occasionally
   - ○ d. Infrequently or never

5. I am within ten pounds of my ideal body weight (please be honest):
   - ○ a. Yes
   - ○ b. No

6. Check the **one response** that best applies to you:

○ a. The foods I eat are mainly determined by convenience and what I feel like eating at the time.

○ b. I attempt to eat fairly good foods most of the time. However, several times a week I end up eating meals that probably aren't very good for me.

○ c. I always (or almost always) attempt to follow a balanced, nutritious diet. I consciously avoid eating excessive amounts of fat, salt and sugar.

7. Do you drink more than two cups of coffee a day, or consume four or more servings of caffeinated tea or cola beverages?

○ a. Yes   ○ b. No

Note on Exercise (for Question 8):

Moderate intensity exercise includes such activities as walking briskly, cycling for pleasure and swimming with a moderate effort.

Vigorous exercise includes such activities as running, tennis, fast cycling and various forms of conditioning exercise such as working out with a stair ergometer or ski machine.

8. Referring to the above guidelines, check the **one response** that best describes your usual level of physical exercise:

○ a. Light or Little Exercise: I rarely engage in moderate intensity or vigorous physical exercise.

○ b. Mild to Moderate Exercise: I engage in moderate intensity exercise for ten to twenty minutes, three or more times a week, or I engage in vigorous exercise one or two times a week (on the average).

○ c. Advanced Moderate to Heavy Exercise: I engage in moderate intensity exercise for thirty minutes or longer at least five times a week, or I engage in vigorous exercise for twenty minutes or longer at least three times a week.

9. I would generally describe the level of stress in my life as:
   - ○ a. Excessive (under heavy stress a lot of the time)
   - ○ b. Moderate
   - ○ c. Relatively low

10. Stress management: I regularly practice some form of daily relaxation ritual, such as meditation, yoga, reflective prayer or another structured mind-quieting activity:
    - ○ a. Yes   ○ b. No

11. Do you smoke cigarettes or other tobacco products?
    - ○ a. Yes   ○ b. No

12. Answer this question *only if you answered "Yes"* to *Question 11.* Do you have definite plans to quit smoking within the next two years?
    - ○ a. Yes   ○ b. No
    - ○ c. Not sure

13. Are you currently married (not separated) or living with a partner in a close, committed relationship?
    - ○ a. Yes   ○ b. No

14. Which of the following best describes your overall level of satisfaction with your relationships with family and friends:
    - ○ a. I am very satisfied with my relationships with family and friends.
    - ○ b. I am moderately satisfied with my relationships with family and friends.
    - ○ c. I am not very satisfied with these relationships.

15. Check the response that best describes how you would rate yourself in reference to the following statement: "My life is characterized by a strong sense of purpose that contributes to a deep sense of fulfillment and enjoyment of life."

○ a. This statement is very true for me.
○ b. This statement is somewhat true for me.
○ c. This statement is not particularly true for me at this point in my life.

16. Which of the following statements best describes your overall level of job satisfaction:
    ○ a. I am very satisfied with my present job.
    ○ b. I am moderately satisfied with my present job.
    ○ c. I am not very satisfied with my present job.
    ○ d. I am not presently employed.

17. In general, how would you rate your overall state of health:
    ○ a. Excellent
    ○ b. Reasonably good
    ○ c. Fair or poor

18. Check the one response that **best applies** to you:
    ○ a. I believe that I have a great deal of control in matters affecting my health.
    ○ b. I believe that I have a moderate degree of control in matters affecting my health.
    ○ c. I believe that I have very little control in matters affecting my health.

19. Check the **one statement** that best applies to you:
    ○ a. I spend a good deal of my time doing things that I really enjoy.
    ○ b. It seems that most of my time is spent doing things that I really don't enjoy.

20. The following statement reflects how some people may feel regarding the spiritual side of life: "I feel comfortable believing in a higher power, or in a sense of meaning in life that is greater than myself."

How would you best describe **your own feelings** about this statement?

○ a. This statement is very true for me.
○ b. This statement is somewhat true for me.
○ c. This statement is not particularly true for me at this point in my life.

Tallying Your Results

Tally your overall wellness index score, using the scoring guide. Beyond your overall score, it may be helpful to reflect on what clues your responses provide regarding your strong points and weak links in reference to wellness planning.

Wellness Lifestyle Assessment Questionnaire Scoring Guide

Instructions: Score your response to each question using the scoring guide presented below and then total your scores. The maximum attainable score is 100. (I've never known anyone who was completely honest and registered a perfect score!) In general, the higher your score, the better off you are in terms of reaping the many benefits of high-level wellness. Be aware, however, that your initial score is only a going-in baseline guide. Start from wherever you are today, commit yourself to wellness—and keep moving in the right direction!

Scoring:

Qs. 1 and 2 are unscored background items.

Q. 3   a = 5, b = 0
Q. 4   a = 5, b = 3, c = 2, d = 0
Q. 5   a = 5, b = 0
Q. 6   a = 0, b = 3, c = 5
Q. 7   a = 0, b = 5
Q. 8   a = 0, b = 5, c = 10
Q. 9   a = 0, b = 3, c = 5   *(continues)*

Q. 10 a = 5, b = 0
Q. 11 a = 0, b = 10
Q. 12 Answer only if you answered "yes" to
       Q.11: a = 4, b = 0, c = 0
Q. 13 a = 5, b = 0
Q. 14 a = 5, b = 3, c = 0
Q. 15 a =10, b = 5, c = 0
Q. 16 a = 5, b = 3, c = 0, d = 3
Q. 17 a = 5, b = 3, c = 0
Q. 18 a = 5, b = 3, c = 0
Q. 19 a = 5, b = 0
Q. 20 a = 5, b = 3, c = 0

Vital Signs and
Health Assessment Worksheet

Name: _____

Date: _____

Age: _____

Basic Wellness Vital Signs:

Body Weight: _____

Height: _____

Body Mass Index: _____

Blood Pressure: _____

Resting Heart Rate: _____

Cholesterol Level: _____

Other Significant Health-Related Indicators
(Screening Tests Results, etc.):

_____

_____

_____

_____

_____

_____

_____

_____

_____

_____

Overall Health Status—
Pinpointing Your Current Strengths
and Weaknesses

Personal Health History/Health-Related Behaviors:

Strong Points: _____

_____

_____

_____

Weak Links: _____

_____

_____

_____

Family Health History:

Strong Points: _____

_____

_____

_____

Weak Links: _____

_____

_____

_____

Longevity Goal

- How long would you **ideally** like to live, if you could reach this age in a relatively robust state of health? _____

_____

- Realistically, how long do you **expect** to live, if you make no changes in your present lifestyle? _____

- What steps immediately come to mind that you can take to **bridge the gap** between these two figures?

  1. _____
  2. _____
  3. _____
  4. _____

Immediate Wellness Goals

- **What immediate improvements** would you like to accomplish in order to positively impact your overall state of health?

  1. _____
  2. _____
  3. _____
  4. _____

12

Action Planning for Wellness: Getting Started, Monitoring Your Progress and Following Through

Using the wellness assessment that you completed in the previous chapter, you are now ready to chart your pathway to optimal health. In this chapter you will complete your Wellness Planning Worksheet. It will summarize your desired life expectancy, long-range wellness goals and immediate wellness objectives, and identify the action steps you will take to transform these goals into reality. You will then move forward to the execution phase, actively tackling the immediate objectives that are most important to you, while monitoring your progress along the way.

Your Wellness Planning Worksheet

At the end of this chapter you will find your Wellness Planning Worksheet. You will use this worksheet to zero in on your long-range wellness goals, followed by tangible short-range goals, immediate wellness objectives and related action steps.

Prior to completing your Wellness Planning Worksheet, I encourage you to take a few moments to review chapter 3—particularly the chart entitled "Factors Influencing a Person's Health," and the discussions pertaining to the Wellness-Illness Continuum, the Dimensions of Wellness and the many parallels between striving to attain high-level wellness and working your 12-step recovery program.

Next, refer to the Wellness Lifestyle Assessment Questionnaire and Vital Signs and Health Assessment Worksheet that you completed in the previous chapter. These guides will provide valuable clues for identifying both your long-range wellness goals and your more immediate objectives and formulating an action plan to take you through the execution phase.

Your Basic Wellness Planning Process

In the wellness planning process you are about to complete, you will start with the "big picture" and proceed to break this down into manageable components. First, you will identify a series of long-range wellness goals that you ultimately aspire to attain. Within this framework, you will then identify your short-range goals for the next twelve months. Once you have zeroed in on these short-range goals, you will then commit yourself to a series of tangible, immediate objectives to accomplish over the next three months. For each of these immediate objectives, you will also specify a sequence of associated action steps.

Let's move on to identifying your long-range wellness goals.

Your Long-Range Wellness Goals

Before completing your Wellness Planning Worksheet, make several copies for future reference. This is critically important, as you will redo this assessment on a quarterly basis to evaluate how well you're accomplishing your short-range wellness objectives, within the broader framework set by your long-range goals. In addition, you will need to revisit your overall wellness goals and execution strategies periodically when you conduct your annual wellness reevaluation.

At the top of the worksheet, fill in the basic background data, together with your longevity goal (taken from your Health Assessment Worksheet).

Next, review your responses to the Wellness Lifestyle Assessment Questionnaire and your Health Assessment Worksheet (from chapter 11), and identify your long-range wellness goals—the milestones that you want to attain in your quest for high-level wellness. These should represent *essential* goals that you plan to realize—the proverbial pot of gold at the end of the rainbow. In addition to identifying your long-range goals in the realm of physical health, be sure to address whatever goals ring true for you in terms of personal fulfillment and bringing greater balance to your life.

For the sake of illustration, I'll share with you some highlights from this section of my own Wellness Planning Worksheet. Later, we'll look at some case studies showing how you can custom-tailor the planning process to your special set of circumstances. In completing my own worksheet at age sixty-one, I identified my longevity goal as over ninety years. I then identified three long-range goals concerned with maximizing my physical health status, as well as several basic goals centered on personal fulfillment and quality of life. Under the category of physical health enhancement, I identified the following long-range goals:

- To live at least thirty more years in a robust state of physical health with maximum energy and alertness.
- To strengthen my immune system and provide the full measure of natural protection against colds, flu and other viruses.
- To maximize my cardiovascular fitness through more fully adopting Dean Ornish's recommendations for a health optimization diet, placing major emphasis on plant-based food sources.

In the realms of personal fulfillment and balance, I identified two important goals:

- To publish a series of books on wellness and recovery, and to promote high-level wellness among as many people as I can reach through my career as a writer, wellness counselor and wellness advocate.
- To achieve a greater degree of balance in my life through broadening my social support system and enriching my relationships with my wife and family—in particular, creating space for more of the "fun things" that Ann and I both enjoy.

Your Short-Range Wellness Goals

Your short-range wellness goals for the next twelve months should be driven by your long-range wellness goals, reflecting those wellness priorities that are of greatest importance to you over the next twelve months. In crystallizing your short-range wellness goals, you need to hone in on concrete, priority-driven measures that appear to be manageable within a twelve-month period.

For the sake of illustration, let's consider the case of Joy, a recovering alcoholic who is a busy working mother in her early thirties with two small children. In addition to wanting to lose some weight herself, she has noticed that her children are already getting chubby—which she attributes to their spending too much time watching TV and playing with the computer. In focusing on her long-range wellness goals, Joy identified two predominant themes. In her words these are:

1. Getting off the fast lane and creating more quality time for both myself and my family.
2. Getting into better physical shape so I can enjoy more energy and feel better about myself.

Flowing from these overriding long-range goals, Joy went on to identify her short-range wellness goals for the next twelve months:

1. **Quality of life:** To work with my husband to pay off our credit card debt over the next year so we can pursue more leisure time as a family, free from the burden of excessive debt.
2. **Quality of life:** To negotiate with my boss concerning cutting my hours back to four days a week, as soon as we've made a substantial dent in our credit card debt.
3. **Quality of life/fitness:** To introduce my children to the joys of physical exercise and sound nutrition and give them a head start in adopting a wellness lifestyle.

4. **Quality of life/fitness:** To identify local, free or low-cost outdoor activities that we can enjoy as a family—and go on a family outing in nature at least every other weekend.
5. **Weight loss/fitness:** To lose twenty-five pounds over the next year—through a combination of cleaning up my nutritional act and regular exercise.

Notice that the short-range goals Joy has identified flow logically from her overriding long-range wellness goals. Within this framework, she has zeroed in on a series of concrete and manageable short-range goals, designed to move both her and her family in the direction identified by her long-range wellness plan.

Immediate Objectives and Action Steps

Now that you have identified your short-range wellness goals for the next twelve months, you need to zero in on your *immediate objectives for the next three months* and formulate an appropriate action plan. These immediate objectives should flow from your short-range wellness goals for the next twelve months. Using your planning worksheet, identify a manageable set of objectives that you can tackle over the next three months. Once you have identified these objectives, you then need to set forth a series of concrete action steps in relation to each objective.

To use another example, I'll share with you one of the immediate objectives from my own Wellness Planning Worksheet. This particular objective provides a good illustration of the pragmatic side of action planning for wellness and the importance of going with the flow in relation to new challenges that life brings our way.

Coincidentally, while I was in the process of completing this chapter, I suffered a hiking injury in which I fractured several ribs. Therefore, in completing this portion of my worksheet, I stated my first immediate objective as follows:

Objective (immediate): To heal from my recent hiking injury as rapidly and naturally as possible.

Underneath this objective, I listed the following action steps:

1. Listen to Emmett Miller's audiotape "Changing the Channel on Pain" on a daily basis and phase myself back into exercise.
2. Locate an acupuncturist and experiment with acupuncture as a vehicle for facilitating my healing process.
3. Continue an appropriate, short-term regimen of pain medication, checking in with my internist, acupuncturist and myotherapist as needed. (A myotherapist is a practitioner specializing in deep tissue massage to alleviate chronic muscular tension.)
4. Facilitate an early return to work by negotiating with my boss a modified work schedule, enabling me to do some of my work at home over the next several weeks.

As it turns out, this sequence of action steps was very helpful in facilitating my objective of healing from this injury as rapidly and naturally as possible. The Emmett Miller audiotape was a godsend during the first several days of intensive pain and helped me get through this period without excessive reliance on pain medication. I was able to immediately resume my daily walking routine, although I found it necessary to pace myself and take several days to build back up to my previous level of forty-five minutes a day. Listening to my body, I discovered that I had to discontinue several of the yoga postures I normally practice for the next several months, as they were aggravating my injury. My myotherapy practitioner coached me by telephone and helped me zero in on a modified regimen of flexibility exercises that enabled me to allow my ribs to fully heal.

At the psychological level, I derived tremendous benefit from negotiating a modified work schedule. The plan we worked out gave me the option of doing a fair amount of work at home during the first several weeks that my ribs were healing. As it turns out, I was able to return to the office full-time after a few days of bed rest. However, by negotiating the possibility of doing some of my work from home, I freed myself from worrying over the possibility of exacerbating my injury by returning to work too soon.

For another illustration of an immediate wellness objective and associated action steps, let's turn again to Joy, the busy working mother with two small children. As you may recall, Joy places a premium on the qualitative aspects of wellness, and she fervently wants to get out of the fast lane and create more quality time for herself and her family. Along these lines, one of the key goals she has identified for the next twelve months is to work with her husband to pay off their credit card debt so they can enjoy more leisure time together as a family free from the burden of excessive debt. Flowing from this twelve-month goal, she has identified the following short-range objective:

Objective: To reduce our credit card debt from $6,000 to $3,000 over the next three months—while at the same time bringing ourselves closer together as a family.

Underneath this objective, Joy has listed the following action steps:

1. Immediately cancel all our credit cards—except for one card that we will only use for true emergencies (such as unanticipated car repairs).
2. Immediately write a check for $1,000 to the credit card company at the beginning of each month, as we are paying our first stack of bills.
3. Put off buying any new clothes until we've reduced our credit card balance to $3,000.
4. Curb our family's expenses by eating out only once a week and instead prepare more nutritious, whole foods–based meals at home. Involve the kids in meal preparation, making this a family project and helping them learn more about sound nutrition.
5. Cut back on expenses by taking family hikes in nature on weekends and making more trips to the beach (bringing a picnic lunch), rather than going to expensive theme parks.

Note that Joy's action steps all support her immediate objective of cutting her family's credit card debt in half over the next three months through a combination of applied discipline and voluntary simplicity. Also note that all of these steps are manageable within the three-month time frame. She has also managed to build into this process a number of creative ways of promoting further bonding within her family, while simultaneously exposing her children to the benefits of outdoor exercise and nutritious food choices.

The above examples should give you some ideas about how you can focus in on your own immediate wellness priorities and related action steps. Remember to let your short-range wellness goals for the next twelve months guide you. In addition, you should try to strike a balance between actions directed towards improving your physical health and actions aimed at fostering greater personal fulfillment and balance in your life.

Your Weekly Review Sheet

In monitoring your progress in achieving your wellness objectives and associated action steps, I encourage you to track your progress on a weekly basis, using the Weekly Review Sheet (which follows the Wellness Planning Worksheet). Depending on your preference, you can use either the short form or the long form (and you don't even need to worry about triggering an IRS audit!). Again, be sure to make several copies of the review sheet before using the form, so that you can use it in the future to track your progress.

The Execution Phase: Taking Charge of Your Health

You are now ready to move into the execution phase, guided by the wellness and longevity blueprint that you created on your Wellness Planning Worksheet. As is the case with working your recovery program, "easy does it" and taking this phase "one day at a time" should be your guiding principles.

I strongly encourage you to jot down your immediate wellness objectives/action steps on your Weekly Review Sheet. Then, at the end of each week, take a few minutes to complete the "How am I doing?" section for each objective and action step.

As an example, let's return to our busy working mother, Joy. You will recall that one of her goals is to lose twenty-five pounds over the next twelve months. Flowing from this goal, she has identified an immediate objective of losing ten pounds within the next three months. Now, let's assume that you share Joy's objective of losing ten pounds over the next three months. This is certainly a realistic goal—if you commit yourself to a reasonable plan for cutting back on calories while simultaneously increasing your exercise level. In our example, for purposes of meeting this immediate wellness objective, you (and Joy) may have identified the following action steps:

- Enroll in a weight-loss class with my health plan
- Cut my desserts back to twice a week
- Plan my daily menus with input from my weight-loss class instructor
- Keep a daily log of my food intake to monitor my progress
- Increase my expenditure of calories by walking—starting out with ten minutes a day and building up to thirty minutes a day by the end of the three-month period.

Using the long form version of the Weekly Review Sheet, you can quickly evaluate at the end of each week how well you are doing. For example: Have you enrolled in the weight-loss class (and are you attending classes)? How many desserts did you actually consume this past week? How are you doing with your walking program? You can also "weigh in" at the end of the week and enter that weight on your review sheet.

The advantage of using your Weekly Review Sheet is that it

enables you to monitor your progress over the short term, celebrate all of the small victories along the way and immediately institute appropriate "course corrections" when you find you are getting off track.

In addition to monitoring your progress via your review sheet, you might also want to augment your individual efforts by working with a wellness sponsor or a supportive friend, joining a wellness support group, or working with a wellness coach. If you are currently in psychotherapy, discuss your wellness goals and action plans with your therapist and ask what he or she can do to support you in this process.

As I have emphasized throughout this book, wellness is a lifelong process. Every living creature thrives on positive reinforcement. Therefore, throughout the execution phase I encourage you to dream up creative ways to reward yourself when you reach important milestones along the way. Examples of major milestones include successfully quitting smoking or attaining your weight loss goal—both of which represent important accomplishments that call for a major celebration.

Equally important, be sure to strive for balance. Find creative ways for making the process fun; this will motivate you to "stay with the program." Be sure to share both your progress and setbacks with other members of your recovery-focused support group, and offer your support and encouragement to them in pursuing their own wellness goals.

Your Quarterly Wellness Assessment and Annual Reevaluation

Three months from today's date, you will conduct your first quarterly wellness assessment. Mark that date on your calendar now. On that date, you will evaluate how well you have accomplished your short-range wellness objectives, noting both your progress and any obstacles you encountered. You will then set new short-range objectives, together with appropriate action steps. Use the Immediate Objectives portion of your Wellness Planning Worksheet to commit these new objectives to writing. Your new objectives and related action steps should reflect your plan over the next three months to further your journey towards high-level wellness. Be sure to retake your quarterly wellness assessment at three-month intervals.

On or about your one-year anniversary date of launching your wellness program, you should set aside several hours to conduct your first annual wellness reevaluation. At this point, you should redo your Wellness Lifestyle Assessment Questionnaire and Health Assessment Worksheet, noting any changes in your Wellness Index Score and Wellness Vital Signs that have occurred over the past year. Hopefully, you will see that a number of positive trends are beginning to emerge!

When you have your annual or semiannual physical examination with your primary care physician, be sure to discuss your wellness goals and action plans with your doctor and elicit his or her input and support. Most physicians will be strongly supportive of patients who are playing an active role in taking charge of their health.

After you have redone your Lifestyle Assessment Questionnaire and Health Assessment Worksheet and reflected on whatever advice your physician has offered, you will then be ready to complete your *new* Wellness Planning Worksheet. When you do this, I strongly encourage you to reevaluate your long-range wellness goals—hopefully with an eye toward raising the bar based on tangible progress that you have witnessed over the past year. Next, identify a new set of short-range goals for the next twelve months, together with a series of immediate objectives and action steps for the next three months.

Remember: Just as your program of recovery from your primary addiction represents a lifelong journey of growth and discovery, your personal commitment to a wellness-oriented lifestyle is an ongoing process of growth and unfolding. Enjoy the journey and reward yourself—frequently—along the way.

Wellness Planning Case Studies

Following are a series of wellness-planning case studies, designed to illustrate how you can customize your action planning for wellness to dovetail with your unique goals, aspirations and individual circumstances.

JOE

Joe is a recovering alcoholic/addict in his midforties who smokes a pack and a half of cigarettes a day and is thirty pounds overweight. His father, who was also a heavy smoker, died from lung cancer in his early fifties, and Joe is determined to avoid following in his footsteps.

In completing his Wellness Planning Worksheet, Joe identified his primary long-range goal as living to age eighty-five so he can see his children get their lives together, enjoy having a good chunk of leisure time to spend with his wife and grandchildren, and pursue his hobbies during his retirement years.

In terms of short-range goals, Joe's primary objective is to successfully quit smoking. After he has kicked the habit and remained tobacco-free for at least six months, he would then like to embark on a structured weight-loss program.

In regard to action steps to support his immediate objective of giving up smoking, Joe identified the following:

- *Discuss my plans to quit smoking with my doctor and explore whether he feels that nicotine replacement therapy is advisable.*
- *Enroll in a smoking-cessation support group.*
- *Set a quit date, follow through with it and stay in frequent contact with my support group members to help me get "over the hump."*

Concurrent with his strategic plans for quitting smoking, Joe is also planning to begin a regular exercise program—in part, because he hopes it will provide an effective substitute activity for smoking. He is planning to start walking fifteen minutes a day— building up to thirty to forty-five minutes a day over the course of his initial three-month wellness-planning time frame. During these first three months, Joe is also planning to explore various approaches to meditation, as he would like to "do something to help calm my restless mind."

In summary, Joe's case provides an excellent example of identifying concrete wellness goals, setting sound priorities and zeroing in on a realistic plan of attack. Notice that while Joe is conscious of his desire to shed the excess baggage from his waistline, he has determined that he wants to first free himself from his nicotine addiction and remain tobacco-free for six months. After he has reached this milestone, he then intends to tackle his weight-loss goals in earnest by participating in a structured weight-loss program. This is probably quite wise, as it is generally best to get some initial successes under our belt and build on that momentum, rather than trying to take on everything at once.

SAM

Sam's case is illustrative of wellness planning centered on the underlying theme of honoring and embracing one's central purpose in life.

Sam is a recovering alcoholic/addict in his late thirties who is a successful tax accountant. Although he is quite comfortable financially, he is acutely aware that he is rather "burnt out" with this line of work. In fact, reflecting on his heavy drinking before joining AA seven years ago, Sam believes that his dissatisfaction with his work was a definite contributing factor to his excessive drinking and drug use.

Sam is currently undergoing psychotherapy, and he has recently been getting in touch with his lifelong love for animals and his earlier dream of becoming a veterinarian. Sam's immediate wellness priorities include doing some volunteer work at a local zoo, while concurrently researching a possible career shift that will enable him to directly express his love for animals. He is planning to investigate options for enrolling in a veterinary college, and he is also going to explore the prospects of opening up a pet store. In addition, he is considering hiring one or more student assistants to help him during this year's tax season to free up more of his own time for actively pursuing a career shift.

In terms of immediate priorities in the realm of physical health, Sam is planning to take up bike riding—biking after work several nights a week as well as on weekends. He is also planning to begin transitioning toward a semivegetarian diet, with the eventual goal of becoming a vegetarian. In addition to the anticipated health benefits, his desire to become a vegetarian is fueled by his intense love for animals.

ELLEN

Ellen is a recovering alcoholic and breast cancer survivor in her early fifties. Looking back over her ordeal with cancer, she appreciates the personal growth that she realized through this experience in terms of perseverance, gutsiness and strengthening her relationship with her higher power. Her healing process also motivated her to pay closer attention to her diet and to take up jogging and yoga.

One of Ellen's immediate wellness priorities is to begin working as a volunteer with the local chapter of the American Cancer Society, providing emotional support to women who have been recently diagnosed with breast cancer. She is also planning to enroll in an upper division course in psychology and begin exploring graduate programs in the counseling field. Ellen is very interested in "giving something back" and believes she would like to work professionally as a counselor, helping other people who are struggling with life-threatening illnesses.

In terms of immediate priorities in the realm of physical

*health, Ellen is planning to get back into a regular jogging pro-
gram and to do some fine-tuning in the area of nutrition. She has
resolved to give up red meat and to actively experiment with
adding vegetarian and semi-vegetarian recipes to her repertoire.*

*In summary, Ellen's case provides a prime example of using an
illness as a learning experience to open the door to new vistas of
personal growth and loving service.*

Dealing With Special Circumstances

Wellness is ultimately concerned with maximizing the quality
of our lives, irrespective of whatever health-related challenges we
may face. Many recovering alcoholics and addicts are indeed
faced with special health challenges. These may include chronic
conditions, such as heart disease, hypertension, diabetes and
chronic fatigue syndrome, as well as cancer, HIV and other life-
threatening illnesses. One of the cornerstones of wellness is
learning to reframe our perceptions regarding any health-related
challenges and adopt a perspective that enables us to respect and
honor our illness as a valuable teacher.

In truth, virtually any illness offers us valuable lessons. Illness
often has a way of showing us areas of our lives that are out of
balance. This, in turn, can point the way towards shifts that we
may need to make in our attitudes and behavior, in the interest
of achieving a greater sense of harmony and balance. The experience of coping with a particularly challenging illness can also
pave the way to new vistas of growth in terms of strength of character, resiliency and increased compassion for others.

In the wellness planning case studies presented earlier in this
chapter, Ellen's story provides a prime example of how a

life-threatening illness can lead one through a positive transformational experience. As a breast cancer survivor, Ellen has a very strong motivation to help others as she prepares for a career as a counselor, in the hope that she will be able to assist other patients who are struggling with life-threatening illnesses.

The life of John F. Kennedy provides a compelling illustration of one man's ability to rise above the challenges posed by a lifelong onslaught of devastating medical problems. Despite the robust "picture of health" image that his publicity staff worked so hard to promote, in actuality Kennedy was plagued by severe health problems and unrelenting pain and physical suffering throughout most of his lifetime. Medical complications that he endured as a youth and throughout his political career included Addison's disease (marked by severe adrenal insufficiency), ulcers, colitis and unrelenting back pain stemming from severe vertebrae damage that virtually disabled him at numerous points in his career. Despite the serious physical health challenges that plagued him, Kennedy was driven by an overriding sense of optimism and personal mission, and he went on to become one of the most charismatic presidents our country has ever witnessed.

On a more personal level, several years ago I witnessed the tremendous courage and strength of character that my brother-in-law, Charlie, portrayed while struggling with terminal lung cancer. A recovering alcoholic and former chain smoker, Charlie was diagnosed with lung cancer in his midsixties. Unfortunately, by the time the doctors detected the illness, the cancer had spread throughout his body. During his final months of coping with this devastating illness, Charlie developed a very close relationship with his higher power, focused his attention on building bridges with various members of his family and stayed incredibly active right up to the end. Just weeks before his passing, he traveled several hundred miles to visit his daughter and her husband in Las Vegas, and he continued to play an active role as president of his trade association in helping them plan their upcoming annual conference. The courage and resiliency that my brother-in-law demonstrated during his final months spoke volumes in terms of the lessons that he imparted to me and other members of his family.

The point I am trying to make here is that the primary determinant of wellness is our quality of life—over and above our physical health per se. Whatever immediate health challenges we may be faced with, we can still take charge of our health and program ourselves for high-level wellness. Indeed, illness can serve as a valuable teacher by pointing the way to necessary lifestyle changes, as well as fostering a deeper appreciation of the many blessings that life has to offer.

Congratulations! You have made major strides along your pathway to optimal health. Based on the wellness planning exercises you completed here and in the preceding chapter, you now have a full kit of exciting wellness tools at your disposal. You are now ready to move forward on a day-to-day basis, while monitoring your progress along the way. As you do so, I encourage you to celebrate your accomplishments—and continue to raise the bar—as you conduct your periodic wellness assessments.

One of the keys to maximizing your prospects for attaining optimal health centers on forming a constructive alliance with your personal physician and other health care professionals. This is the focus of the next chapter.

Wellness Planning Worksheet

Name: _____

Date: _____

Age: _____

Longevity Goal:

Ideal age you'd like to attain: _____

Long Range Wellness Goals:

Identify your long-range wellness goals—landmarks that you want to attain in your personal quest for high-level wellness. In defining your goals, be sure to address goals that are important to you in the area of personal fulfillment, as well as in the arena of optimal health.

1. _____
   _____
   _____

2. _____
   _____
   _____

3. _____
   _____
   _____

4. _____
   _____
   _____

5. _____
   _____
   _____

Short Range Wellness Goals—
Immediate Objectives

Short-Range Goals for Next Twelve Months:

1. _____
2. _____
3. _____

Immediate Wellness Objectives for Next Three Months and Related Action Steps:

Time Frame: _____

1. Objective _____
Action Steps:

_____

_____

_____

2. Objective _____
Action Steps:

_____

_____

_____

3. Objective _____
Action Steps:

_____

_____

_____

Action Planning for Wellness
Weekly Review Sheet—Short Form

Immediate Objectives and Action Steps

Objective No. 1: _____

_____

How am I doing? _____

_____

_____

Objective No. 2: _____

_____

How am I doing? _____

_____

_____

Objective No. 3: _____

_____

How am I doing? _____

_____

_____

Overall Comments/Course Corrections: _____

_____

_____

_____

Action Planning for Wellness
Weekly Review Sheet—Long Form

Immediate Wellness Objective: _____

_____

Action Step No. 1: _____

_____

How am I doing? _____

_____

_____

Action Step No. 2: _____

_____

How am I doing? _____

_____

_____

Action Step No. 3: _____

_____

How am I doing? _____

_____

_____

Overall Comments/Course Corrections: _____

_____

_____

_____

CHAPTER

13

Making Optimal Use
of Health Care Resources

As a person in recovery, there are many reasons you should learn to make wise use of doctors and other health care resources. You have suffered the consequences of years of excessive drinking and drug use in terms of chronic nutritional imbalances, and you may have sustained significant damage to your body's organs. Chances are, while you were in the active stages of your addiction, you were not particularly adept at checking in with your physician for periodic physical examinations or following through on your doctor's advice. In fact, you may have even avoided seeing your doctor, out of fear that he or she might "blow your cover" and try to get you into treatment.

Now that you are in recovery, it definitely behooves you to give caring for your body at least the same priority that you would place on taking care of your car. This means following your body's "maintenance manual" and obtaining treatment for any existing medical problems. You also should take full advantage of the various preventative services that modern medicine provides. Forming an ongoing relationship with a personal physician who has some familiarity with addictive disorders can also be helpful in keeping you on the right path in terms of relapse prevention.

My goal in this chapter is to give you some very practical pointers for effectively using doctors and other health care resources to your advantage, paying particular attention to the special needs and concerns of people in recovery. By way of background, let's first take a brief look at some of the more troubling features of our nation's health care system.

America's Troubled Health Care System

From the perspective of promoting optimal health, America's health care system is wired backwards. By this I mean that the majority of our health care resources are poured into providing very expensive, high-tech interventions focusing on end-stage illness, rather than on actively encouraging patients to stay healthy by empowering them to take charge of their health.

Our health care system has a chemical dependency problem of its own, combined with a hard-core addiction to excessive technological intervention. America's health care system is clearly dominated by the pharmaceutical industry, which underwrites the lion's share of medical research. The system is also dominated by major medical centers and manufacturers of high-tech medical devices, which stand to realize a hefty profit from a health care system that overutilizes CT scans, MRIs, and other expensive, technologically driven medical and surgical interventions. Within the medical profession, the highest prestige and income has traditionally been accorded to the "high-tech fraternity," including surgical subspecialists, together with radiologists and anesthesiologists. Ironically, family practitioners, pediatricians and other primary care physicians, who are predominantly concerned with working on the frontlines to help us stay healthy, have been relegated to the bottom of the pecking order in terms of both income and status.

The High Cost of Health Care: Who Is to Blame?

One of the most frightening phenomena regarding health care in America is the fact that our health care system has priced itself beyond the reach of a sizable segment of our population. Our nation's health care expenditures reached $1.7 trillion in 2003, gobbling up 15.3 percent of the gross domestic product. Faced with double-digit inflation in health insurance premiums, many businesses are dropping health coverage for their employees. As of this writing, the number of Americans without any form of health insurance totals 44 million, with no end in sight.

In addition to the pressures associated with excessive profit taking, a large share of the blame for our runaway inflation in health care costs rests squarely with you and me as consumers. As a nation, we have embraced lifestyles that are abysmally out of balance: witness our national epidemic of obesity and sedentary behavior. Many, if not most, Americans fail to take care of themselves and simply wait until they become very sick—expecting doctors and hospitals to miraculously patch them up.

Our over-reliance on prescription drugs is particularly

appalling. A recent Kaiser Family Foundation study cites rising costs and consumption of prescription drugs as a driving force behind the current wave of health care inflation. Our nation's expenditures for prescription drugs rose by 15.7 percent between 2000 and 2001, with the typical family of four spending close to $2,000 annually on prescription drugs. In truth, we've become a nation of prescription drug addicts!

Hopefully, as a person in recovery who is committed to taking charge of your health, you will want to give yourself a strong leg up on most Americans in terms of taking care of yourself and making wise use of health care resources. While I firmly believe that as a nation we have become overly reliant on doctors, hospitals and other health care providers, these resources definitely have their place in helping us remain healthy and facilitating healing when we become sick. We just need to keep them in proper perspective and realize that we are ultimately responsible for our state of health.

Using Health Care Resources to Support Your Commitment to Wellness and Recovery

This section is designed to provide practical pointers concerning how you, as a person in recovery, can effectively use doctors and other health care resources to your best advantage. In particular, we discuss the importance of choosing your personal physician wisely, using caution in regard to taking any medications, safeguarding your sobriety in the event of surgery that requires postoperative pain management and exploring the possible role of an addictionologist in rounding out your personal health care team.

Choosing a Primary Care Physician

Choose your primary care physician wisely. No one in their right mind would think of letting a car dealer randomly assign them whatever was in the lot when they were shopping for a new car. Yet many of us would let our health plan or medical group randomly assign us a personal physician without giving it a second thought. There's something wrong with this equation! Your primary care physician is the most important player in your health care team, as he or she is charged with assuming active responsibility for your ongoing health maintenance. It is crucially important that you play a proactive role in structuring this critical alliance. Your goal should be to connect with a primary physician with whom you feel comfortable—preferably someone who has some degree of familiarity with the medical ramifications of recovery from alcoholism and drug addiction.

How do you find such a doctor? One alternative is to contact your local medical society for a referral to a primary care physician who is familiar with addictive disorders. If you are an HMO patient, contact your health plan or medical group for assistance in linking up with an appropriate primary care physician—stressing that you are seeking someone with firsthand experience caring for patients in recovery. Other good referral sources for locating such a doctor include your local 12-step program's central office and fellow 12-steppers. These folks can be very helpful in finding a physician that you will click with, particularly if they are also members of your health plan.

During your initial visit with your primary care doctor, you need to "test the waters." Be sure to disclose your chemical dependency history. A physician cannot help you in this important area unless you share this information with him or her. Also, be particularly observant during your first visit concerning how your new doctor comes across. Does this doctor come across as knowledgeable, personable and genuinely interested in you as a person? Or they appear harried and rushed? Above all, do you feel you can trust this physician at the gut level? If your initial choice of doctor is not panning out for any reason, don't be afraid to request a reassignment.

Medications and Your Recovery

As a person in recovery, you should exercise caution concerning any medications that a physician prescribes or recommends for you, paying particularly close attention to any potential addictive properties that might pose a threat to your sobriety. Quoting from Joseph D. Beasley, M.D., coauthor of *Food for Recovery* and former department chair at the Harvard University School of Public Health:

> . . . [i]ndividuals in recovery must be vigilant about avoiding addictive medications of all kinds and must inform their physicians, dentists, therapists, and so forth of their addictive history. It is not safe to assume that your doctors will ask all the right questions. You must give him or her the information. Always ask about the possible side effects and addictive potential of a prescribed medication, and ask if there are any nonaddictive alternatives. Find out how long you should be taking the medication, and be sure that there is a time limit and a dosage limit. If your doctor or dentist makes light of your concern, try to educate him or her about the realities of recovery.

In addition to prescribed medications, you need to exercise caution about the potential addictive properties associated with both over-the-counter (OTC) medications and herbal remedies. Many OTC medications contain alcohol and other psychoactive substances with addictive potential. A common example is pseudoephedrine hydrochloride—a decongestant that is also a potent stimulant and appetite suppressant.

You also need to be aware that so-called natural remedies are not necessarily completely safe: a number of liquid homeopathic and herbal remedies come in an alcohol base. In addition, as herbal remedies are currently not subject to stringent Food and Drug Administration regulation, a number of dangerous "natural" stimulants with amphetamine-like properties are currently sold by many natural foods stores. A glaring example is the herbal product ephedra—implicated in the death of twenty-three-year-old Baltimore Orioles' pitcher Steve Bechler due to cardiovascular complications—which was recently banned by the federal governmental in an unprecedented move. If you have any doubts whatsoever concerning the potential safety or addictive potential of any OTC medication or herbal remedy, be sure to consult your personal physician or a knowledgeable pharmacist.

Hospitalization and Surgery: A Special Cautionary Note Regarding CNS Drugs and Your Recovery

People in recovery must be particularly cautious about taking any prescribed medication that affects the central nervous system (CNS). These drugs—which can mimic the effects of alcohol and other drugs of choice and are potentially addictive themselves—include pain medications; sedatives and hypnotics (used most often to promote sleep but sometimes in medical procedures as well); and antianxiety drugs such as the benzodiazepines (used mostly to treat anxiety and muscle spasms).

Many people in recovery, despite their best efforts to safeguard against relapse, have returned to drinking and drug use following exposure to CNS drugs in unavoidable medical situations, such as hospitalization associated with surgery or major accidents.

In *Eating Right to Live Sober,* Katherine Ketcham and L. Ann Mueller, M.D., offer very sound advice to recovering alcoholics/addicts about minimizing the potential hazards to sobriety associated with exposure to CNS medications in such situations. They strongly advocate proactively planning a course of "restabilization," in concert with your physician and loved ones, in advance of any elective medical procedure that may involve the use of CNS drugs. The following summary is adapted from their recommendations:

- In the event of elective surgery, it is critically important that you initiate a proactive plan for restabilization, in concert with your physician, before you are exposed to CNS drugs. This is vitally important, as chances are good that you may not be thinking clearly once you are under the influence of these medications.
- Fully discuss your chemical dependency history with your physician and elicit his or her active support to ensure your sobriety maintenance. It may also be wise to request that your physician consult an addictionologist (a physician with special training in addictive disorders).
- If your doctor recommends that you continue use of CNS medications for a few days following surgery or a major

dental procedure, make advance arrangements to ensure that you only take home a limited supply of medication. As the CNS drugs will alter your thought processes, ensure that you will have personal assistance from a trusted source to monitor your use of prescribed medications. Ask if your health plan can authorize temporary home health assistance. If this is not feasible, arrange for a relative or someone else with a strong grounding in sobriety to monitor your in-home use of CNS medication. These measures will serve as a safeguard against succumbing to the temptation to use more drugs (or alcohol) during your initial days of postsurgical recovery.

- As a preventative measure, be sure to alert your family, your sponsor or a close friend about your restabilization plan, in the event that an accident or other unanticipated medical emergency occurs that might result in your being exposed to CNS medications.

The above precautions are particularly applicable to people in the early stages of sobriety. In addition to this very sound advice, I would recommend that you use a good audiocassette tape focusing on preparing your mind and body for surgery, both before and after any elective surgical procedure. Along these lines, I highly recommend the following tapes by Dr. Emmett Miller: *Successful Surgery and Recovery* and *Changing the Channel on Pain*. (See the Appendix at the end of this book for further details.) In addition to fostering a positive mind/body interaction that may facilitate a beneficial surgical outcome, the use of specially formatted audiotapes in conjunction with planned surgery may also prove helpful in reducing your need for pain medication.

Important: If you are contemplating elective surgery, be sure to fully discuss with your surgeon your use of any medications and nutritional supplements, including herbal preparations and vitamin/mineral supplements, to determine which of these items you should discontinue before the scheduled surgery. It is especially important that you disclose your use of any herbal medications, as many of these substances—including echinacea, ephedra, ginkgo biloba, ginseng and St. John's wort—can produce dangerous side effects when combined with the blood-thinning medications commonly used in surgery.

Consider Consulting an Addictionologist

An addictionologist is a physician who has received special training in the identification and treatment of addictive disorders of all kinds, and who has been certified by the American Society of Addiction Medicine. If you have a history of numerous relapses following alcohol/drug treatment, or if you have serious medical complications that might affect your ability to successfully work your recovery program, you may wish to consider establishing an ongoing relationship with an addictionologist as a medical consultant.

The addictionologist's role as medical consultant should not be viewed as a substitute for your relationship with your primary care physician. Rather, the addictionologist should serve as a consultant to both you and your primary doctor regarding medical treatments that may affect your recovery. For example, an addictionologist can answer questions regarding the potential addictive properties of any prescription drugs, over-the-counter medications, and even vitamin and herbal supplements that your doctor or other health care professional may recommend.

An addictionologist can also serve as a valuable second-opinion resource whenever you are faced with medical complications that make it prudent to consult with a doctor who is well-versed in recovery issues. In particular, the addictionologist should be available to consult with you and your primary doctor or dentist about any proposed use of pain medications.

For assistance in locating a certified addictionologist in your area, contact:

The American Society of Addiction Medicine
4601 N. Park Avenue, Upper Arcade #101
Chevy Chase, MD 20815
(301) 656-3920
E-mail: *email@asam.org*

Additional Pointers for Effectively Using Physicians and Health Plans

Today's health care system is extremely difficult for anyone to navigate—and people in recovery are no exception.

If you are fortunate enough to have private health insurance, you are most likely covered by either a health maintenance organization (HMO) or a preferred provider organization (PPO). An HMO is essentially a closed system of doctors, affiliated hospitals and other health care resources in which your primary care doctor controls your access to other health care services by serving as a "gatekeeper." A key advantage associated with HMOs is that by closely managing members' use of health care services, the health plan makes a very focused effort to hold costs down, thus enabling it to offer a relatively rich health benefits package. The flip side is that many patients are turned off by the limited freedom of choice and restrictions pertaining to access to specialty services that go with most HMO arrangements.

Many people who have become disenchanted with the restrictions of HMO coverage have opted for PPO plans. A PPO is designed to provide greater freedom of choice, enabling patients to access doctors and other health care providers both inside and outside the health plan network. In a PPO you also have considerably greater latitude in accessing physician specialists and other health care services on your own, without going through a gatekeeper system. The downside is that PPO coverage can be considerably more expensive in terms of out-of-pocket costs. Typically, employees end up paying the differential between the monthly premium for the PPO plan versus the lower-priced HMO option offered by their employer. Additionally, they shoulder the burden of annual deductibles and copayments ranging from 10 to 20 percent—with even higher copayments applying when you go out of network.

Regardless of which type of health insurance coverage you choose, you need to learn how to work the system to your advantage. The following pointers are designed to help you do this.

Form a Constructive Alliance with Your Primary Care Physician

Form a constructive alliance with your primary care physician and negotiate your plan of care. In any managed care setting, you must be your own foremost health care advocate. Remember that your health plan is a moneymaking business, and as such, their primary goal is to cut costs and make a profit. To make sure you aren't short-changed in the cost-cutting equation, you need to develop an alliance with your doctor and have him or her on your side. Your goal should be to form a relationship with your doctor that is characterized by shared respect and mutual participation in the medical decision-making process. Toward that end, you need to be both diplomatic and constructively assertive.

It is particularly important that you work with your primary care physician to ensure your health care needs are effectively met while at the same time respecting the health plan's legitimate need to control health care costs. Don't just blindly accept your doctor's initial recommendations if they fly in the face of what you believe is best for you. Become an active and fully informed participant in the decision-making process and engage your doctor in exploring the full range of available treatment options. Remember that you are seeking to promote the best possible health care outcome, in line with your personal wellness goals.

Make the Best Use of the Ten-Minute Doctor-Patient Encounter

In today's hectic health care environment, most doctor-patient encounters typically run ten minutes or less. Being aware of this reality can empower you to make the best possible use of the limited time available.

Be focused. In preparation for your visit, take a few minutes and write down:

- Your key complaints and concerns
- Your thoughts concerning what is going on

- Any relevant personal or family health history that relates to your current complaint
- Your going-in thoughts as to possible treatment options
- The key questions that you are seeking answers to

During the visit, be an active participant. Talk with your doctor. Fully discuss the various treatment alternatives relating to your particular problem and be sure to make your preferences known. Immediately following your visit, take a moment to write down a summary of the key points that you and the doctor agreed to, paying particular attention to any recommended follow-up treatment, self-care measures and/or lifestyle modifications.

Take Full Advantage of Your Health Plan's Preventative Service Offerings

Think about it: If your body came with an owner's manual, would you take the time to read it? In terms of preventative maintenance, most of us take better care of our cars than we do of our own bodies. If you are like many people in recovery, you may be carrying a lot of health-related baggage from your years of drinking and drugging. Time to check out that owner's manual!

The older we get, the more important it is to follow a sound preventative health maintenance schedule. The good news is that most health plans offer a range of health education classes and support groups. Offerings of relevance to many people in recovery include programs focusing on smoking cessation, nutrition and weight loss, and stress management. Check them out.

Also be sure to take full advantage of your health plan's

screening services for high blood pressure, heart disease, diabetes and many forms of cancer. Discuss with your doctor which screening tests are advisable for someone your age with your personal and family health history. Screening tests are important and can help your doctor detect potentially serious conditions at an early stage when they are most treatable. Health plans like this too, as early detection and treatment saves them money in the end.

Using Special Health Care Resources Wisely

Before concluding our discussion about how to use health care resources to your advantage, we should briefly focus on two topics of importance to many people in recovery—namely, the potential use of growth-oriented psychotherapy, and the ins and outs associated with using alternative health care services.

Growth-Oriented Psychotherapy

Many people reach a point in their recovery where they wish to supplement their 12-step work with either individual or group psychotherapy. The objective here is to get more fully in touch with what they want to do with their lives and transform their dreams into reality.

Growth-oriented psychotherapy can be particularly valuable in helping you develop the skills needed to cope effectively with the many challenges that confront us in today's complex world. This type of therapy can also help you fully express your potential as a unique person. Many people in recovery also find that psychotherapy helps anchor them by helping them navigate the various "identity crises" that life confronts them with.

Growth-centered therapy can also help you develop the resilience needed to cope more effectively with highly stressful situations.

If you are considering becoming involved in psychotherapy, you should seek out a therapist who is sensitive to recovery-focused issues and will actively support your recovery program. Concurrently, your therapist should serve as a catalyst in stretching your horizons relative to those areas of growth that are most important to you. Take care to link up with a therapist whom you genuinely respect—ideally, this should be someone whom you can see as an effective role model. If you are fortunate enough to find a therapist who shares your commitment to high-level wellness, ask your therapist if he or she would be willing to double as a wellness coach to help you stay on track in terms of pursuing optimal health and personal fulfillment.

How does one find a good therapist to work with, and how do you go about getting the most out of the therapeutic relationship? As the process of therapy is highly personalized, word of mouth referrals can be very helpful. Your sponsor, other members of your recovery network, or a friend or relative who has had a positive experience with psychotherapy are all potential referral sources. Other valuable sources include your health plan, the employee assistance program at your place of work and the various professional associations representing licensed psychotherapists.

Ideally, before committing yourself to working with a therapist, you should narrow your search down to several prospective candidates and interview them by telephone. Describe the issues that you want to work on, and ask how they would propose to help you. It is critically important that both you and the therapist reach accord concerning therapeutic goals and the likely course of treatment. Also discuss the costs of treatment, and determine if the therapist is a participating provider with your health plan. When interviewing the therapist by telephone, be particularly sensitive to the chemistry between you, and ask yourself if this is someone with whom you would feel comfortable working. Over and above the therapist's professional credentials, the most important ingredients in any effective therapeutic relationship are trust, your level of comfort in working with the therapist and your overall level of confidence in his or her ability to help you. Above all else, trust your gut.

A Sane Slant on Alternative Medicine

Alternative approaches to health care—that is, healing methods that depart from conventional Western medicine—have enjoyed an unprecedented wave of popularity over the past decade. According to a widely quoted study published in the *New England Journal of Medicine*, the amount of money spent by Americans on various forms of alternative treatment currently exceeds the total outlay for visits to primary care physicians.

Some of the more popular alternative healing modalities include chiropractic, massage therapy, traditional Chinese medicine (including acupuncture), traditional ayurvedic medicine, naturopathic medicine and guided imagery. In addition to seeking out alternative health treatments when confronted with various physical illnesses, growing numbers of people struggling with addictive disorders are turning to acupuncture, yoga, massage therapy, guided imagery and other alternative offerings to ease their withdrawal symptoms and help them obtain a fuller grounding in the early stages of sobriety.

In contrast with the intensely technological orientation of contemporary Western medicine—with its heavy emphasis on drugs, surgery and other high-tech interventions—alternative health practitioners purport to follow a more natural, gentler path to healing that seeks to facilitate the body's own healing processes, while honoring the interplay of mind, body and spirit in health and illness.

When treating an illness, alternative practitioners attempt to approach the problem at the root cause level, focusing on underlying imbalances in the patient's life in such areas as diet and exercise, together with how the person relates to the world around them. Rather than relying on conventional pharmacological or surgical interventions, alternative practitioners will typically prescribe various herbal supplements and megavitamins, which purportedly function to build upon and strengthen the body's natural healing processes. Alternative practitioners also tend to place fairly heavy reliance on various forms of energy flow manipulation—such as acupuncture, reflexology or therapeutic massage—in an effort to facilitate a more harmonious state of balance within the body and channel healing energies to the bodily systems that are experiencing distress.

Should you incorporate the offerings of alternative medicine into your own pursuit of high-level wellness? The answer depends largely on your own philosophy, together with your comfort zone in reference to conventional Western medicine versus the more experimental methods associated with alternative healing approaches. Phrasing it differently—are you completely satisfied with the results obtained through conventional medical treatment for your health problems, or might you also be interested in exploring potential benefits associated with various forms of alternative treatment?

Over the years I have personally benefited from a number of alternative healing therapies, including chiropractic, guided imagery, yoga, transcendental meditation, various herbal and homeopathic remedies, and myotherapy—a discipline that integrates deep-tissue, trigger-point massage with a structured regimen of self-care, designed to counteract chronic muscular tension.

As such, I am a firm believer in an integrative approach to health care that seeks to blend both conventional and alternative treatments. If your primary care physician fully honors your commitment to taking charge of your health and is open-minded about various alternative healing options, then you are indeed fortunate. When you are confronted with a health challenge that is not fully responding to conventional medical treatment, you should be able to call upon a team of both conventional and alternative practitioners who will work together to produce the best possible healing outcome for you as the patient.

How do you go about finding an appropriate alternative practitioner to work with? The self-help section of your local bookstore and the various Internet search engines can serve as useful starting points. Begin by actively researching your problem, with the objective of pinpointing those treatment options, both conventional and alternative, that make the most sense to you. Once you have identified an alternative healing modality that appeals to you, begin to search for a practitioner who is skilled in that discipline. Many alternative disciplines, including acupuncture, homeopathy, naturopathic medicine, reflexology and hypnotherapy, have established national certifying agencies that screen practitioners and ensure that they meet certain minimal qualifications. In addition, naturopathic physicians and doctors of traditional Chinese medicine are licensed in many states. You can probably link up with the applicable licensure or certifying agency online and elicit their help in locating a qualified practitioner in your area.

Word of mouth referrals can be very helpful in narrowing down your search. A referral from a patient who has had an exceptionally positive experience with the type of practitioner that you are seeking can be worth its weight in gold. And don't overlook your local natural food store. Staffs of these outlets tend to be very health conscious, and they often have a line on practitioners in your community who are particularly effective and ethical.

Once you have identified a prospective practitioner to work with, I would recommend that you interview them by telephone before scheduling an appointment. Ask them to describe their qualifications and credentials, outline for them your problem and the type of help you are seeking, and ask them what their treatment approach would be. Ask for specifics regarding their own base of experience in treating this particular problem. Better still, ask if they can give you the telephone number of a patient with a similar problem whom they have treated.

Assess the chemistry, to determine whether you would feel comfortable working with this practitioner. Also discuss their fees, and ask them to estimate the probable length of treatment. Unfortunately, many alternative health practices are not currently covered by health insurance, which means you will need to cover the costs of treatment out of pocket. Ask the practitioner if he or she offers a sliding fee scale, and work together to negotiate a fee structure that is fair and equitable to both sides.

To wind up this section, let me reiterate that you are in charge of your health. You must place yourself squarely in the driver's seat and make appropriate use of doctors and other health care resources to help you along the way. That being said, I hope that I have succeeded in whetting your appetite for actively exploring the potential benefits of both conventional and alternative healing.

If you are intrigued by the prospect of working with an alternative healer, I encourage you to seek out a reputable and trustworthy practitioner and enjoy the experience—while keeping your eyes wide open. Be guided by your curiosity and sense of adventure, together with a healthy mind-set of scientific inquiry and skepticism, when that is called for. Do not blindly place your trust in a particular healing modality just because its proponents claim that it is "natural" or "holistic." At all times, listen to what your body is telling you, and be guided by both your intellect and your intuition. Follow the path and enjoy the journey.

Parting Thoughts

C ongratulations!

Over the course of the previous pages, you have chosen to embark on an exciting journey along previously uncharted grounds. If you have actively participated in the various exercises presented in this book, you are well on your way to charting your pathway to optimal health and personal fulfillment.

In the preceding chapters you have learned how to take charge of your health and add years—most likely decades—to your life expectancy. You have also learned how to take control of your destiny and live your life to the fullest. You have been fully exposed to the various dimensions of wellness—including stress management, physical fitness, your nutritional foundation for recovery, and the all-important elements of central purpose, spirituality and life satisfaction. And you have been given the tools to integrate these powerful dimensions into your day-to-day life and your recovery program.

Over the course of the final chapters, you have conducted your personal wellness assessment and begun the exciting process of action planning for wellness. In your action planning process, you have zeroed in on your own wellness goals and priorities, together with the associated action steps. In doing so, you have taken major strides along your personal pathway to optimal health and maximum personal fulfillment.

Where do you go from here? Over the weeks, months and years ahead, I strongly encourage you to actively embrace the guidelines presented in chapter 11, "Conducting Your Personal Wellness Assessment," and in chapter 12, "Action Planning for Wellness," as you forge ahead with your own action plan for wellness. As we discussed in chapter 12, it is my fervent hope that as you move forward, you will monitor your progress, celebrating your successes and continue to raise the bar as you conduct your periodic wellness assessments and reevaluations.

Please note: If you have not yet completed the wellness assessment and action planning exercises outlined in chapters 11 and 12, I urge you to return to these chapters and do these exercises. I really want to see you "get with the program" and make a wholehearted commitment to pursuing high-level wellness now and for the rest of your life.

Hopefully, over the course of this book, I have been able to convince you that wellness is *fun*. I hope that you will choose to join me in embracing wellness as an exciting hobby that promises to open up new vistas of growth, self-actualization and pure enjoyment. I especially want to encourage you to embrace and manifest your unique sense of purpose for being on this planet as an integral component of your personal journey to wellness.

As you continue moving forward on your own journey to optimal health, I hope that you will become motivated to reach out and encourage others to join you. Drawing on an analogy to the 12-step programs, as you begin to achieve major milestones along your own pathway to wellness, such as giving up smoking or shedding excess baggage from your waistline, you may become motivated to take the message to those who are still suffering by encouraging them to adopt a wellness-oriented lifestyle.

One of my dreams is that addiction treatment centers will embrace the wellness and recovery movement and sponsor wellness programs for clients currently undergoing treatment—as well as program alumni. If you have previously completed a treatment program for alcoholism or drug addiction, you may be able to interest your program in organizing a wellness and recovery club for interested alumni. Examples of wellness-oriented programs that centers can sponsor for interested alumni include physical conditioning programs, smoking cessation support groups and discussion/support groups centered on various wellness themes. Such activities can offer real dividends for sponsoring treatment centers through strengthening their continuing care components and reducing the likelihood of relapse.

I would also like to invite you to join me in broadening your personal commitment to wellness by serving as a catalyst to promote wellness both within your own community and at the broader planetary level. As you begin racking up substantial accomplishments along your pathway to optimal health, you may become motivated to become involved in efforts to improve the quality of life in your community. Over the past several years, considerable attention has been focused on the sorry state of American youth in terms of lack of physical fitness, combined with a frightening level of obesity among both preteens and teenagers as a result of eating the wrong foods and failing to exercise. Our public schools and community agencies are desperately in need of committed volunteers who are willing to roll up their sleeves and pitch in to help turn around this sorry state of affairs. Likewise, inner city areas throughout the country are urgently in need of concerned adults who are willing to commit some focused energy on serving as role models for troubled youths and providing them with a viable alternative to street gangs and drug trafficking.

I would also encourage you, either now or at some point in the future, to consider becoming involved in environmental activism. The Sierra Club, Greenpeace and other environmental activist organizations will gladly welcome whatever assistance you can lend to their efforts to clean up our environment and tackle a barrage of serious environmental hazards that threaten the very livability of our planet. These challenges include, among others, the pollution of our oceans and rivers and the air that we breathe, global warming and depletion of the ozone layer.

Other examples of worthy causes promoting wellness at the planetary level include lending our efforts to combat worldwide hunger and working as activists to promote worldwide peace. The important thing is to listen to your inner guidance and place your energy behind wherever your calling may take you.

In the Appendix at the end of this book, I present recommended readings and additional resources to stimulate further growth in the area of wellness and recovery. In this section you will find highlights concerning some of my favorite wellness gurus, together with some of my favorite inspirational books, audiocassettes, videotapes, magazines and newsletters focusing on wellness themes. I also invite you to visit my Web site at *www.wellnessandrecovery.com*, for timely pointers and news about upcoming talks and workshops that focus on wellness and recovery.

Once again, my congratulations to you on your personal commitment to wellness and recovery. It is my hope and expectation that your journey along the pathway to optimal health will dramatically improve your quality of life, add many years of joyful living to your life span and yield dividends that extend beyond your wildest dreams. To your health!

Appendix

Suggested Resources
for Wellness and Recovery

This directory is intended to serve as a guide to recommended readings and additional resources, which can stimulate further growth in the area of wellness and recovery.

Books, Periodicals and Audiocassettes

This listing includes some of my favorite authors and works that I have found particularly inspirational.

General Wellness

Benson, Herbert. *Timeless Healing: The Power and Biology of Belief.* New York: Scribner, 1996.

Chopra, Deepak. *Ageless Body, Timeless Mind.* New York: Harmony Books, 1993.

Glasser, William. *Positive Addiction.* New York: Harper Collins, 1976.

——. *Warning: Psychiatry Can be Hazardous to Your Mental Health.* New York: Harper Collins, 2003.

Hafen, Brent Q., Keith J. Karren, Kathryn J. Frandsen, and N. Lee Smith. *Mind/Body Health: The Effects of Attitudes, Emotions, and Relationships.* Boston: Allyn and Bacon, 1996.

Mehl-Madrona, Lewis. *Coyote Medicine.* New York: Scribner, 1997.

Miller, Emmett E. *Deep Healing: The Essence of Mind/Body Medicine.* Carlsbad, CA: Hay House, 1997.

Ornish, Dean. *Dr. Dean Ornish's Program for Reversing Heart Disease.* New York: Ballantine, 1990.

———. *Love & Survival: The Scientific Basis for the Healing Power of Intimacy.* New York: Harper Collins, 1998.

Siegel, Bernie S. *Love, Medicine & Miracles.* New York: Harper & Row, 1986.

Theodosakis, Jason, and David T. Feinberg. *Don't Let Your HMO Kill You: How to Wake Up Your Doctor, Take Control of Your Health and Make Managed Care Work for You.* New York: Routledge, 2000.

Travis, John W., and Regina Sara Ryan. *Wellness Workbook.* Berkeley, CA: Ten Speed Press, 2004.

Weil, Andrew. *Spontaneous Healing: How to Discover and Enhance Your Body's Natural Ability to Maintain and Heal Itself.* New York: Alfred A. Knopf, 1995.

———. *Natural Health, Natural Medicine: A Comprehensive Manual for Wellness and Self-Care.* New York: Houghton Mifflin Co., 1998.

———. *Eating Well for Optimum Health: The Essential Guide to Food, Diet, and Nutrition.* New York: Alfred A. Knopf, 2000.

Spiritual Dimension of Wellness and Recovery

Ash, Mel. *The Zen of Recovery.* New York: Jeremy P. Tarcher/Putnam, 1993.

Borg, Marcus, ed. *Jesus and Buddha: The Parallel Sayings.* Berkley, CA: Ulysses Press, 1997.

Chopra, Deepak. *The Seven Spiritual Laws of Success: A Practical Guide to the Fulfillment of Your Dreams.* San Rafael, CA: Amber-Allen Publishing/New World Library, 1994.

Coelho, Paulo. *The Alchemist: A Fable About Following Your Dream.* New York: HarperPerennial, 1988.

Csikszentmihalyi, Mihaly. *Flow: The Psychology of Optimal Experience.* New York: Quality Paperback Book Club by arrangement with HarperCollins Publishers, 1990.

Dalai Lama. *The Path to Tranquility: Daily Wisdom.* New York: Viking Arkana, 1998.

——. *Ethics for the New Millennium.* New York: Riverhead Books, 1999.

Dossey, Larry. *Reinventing Medicine: Beyond Mind-Body to a New Era of Healing.* San Francisco: HarperSanFranciso, 1999.

——. *Healing Beyond the Body: Medicine and the Infinite Reach of the Mind.* Boston: Shambhala, 2001.

Farmer, Steven D. *Sacred Ceremony: How to Create Ceremonies for Healing, Transitions, and Celebrations.* Carlsbad, CA: Hay House, 2002.

Goleman, Daniel, ed. *Healing Emotions: Conversations With the Dalai Lama on Mindfulness, Emotions and Health.* Boston: Shambhala, 1997.

Hillman, James. *The Soul's Code: In Search of Character and Calling.* New York: Random House, 1996.

Le Joly, Edward, and Jaya Chaliha. *Mother Teresa's Reaching Out in Love.* New York: Barnes & Noble Books, 1998.

Millman, Dan. *Way of the Peaceful Warrior: A Book That Changes Lives.* Tiburon, CA: HJ Kramer, 1984.

——. *Everyday Enlightenment: The Twelve Gateways to Personal Growth.* New York: Warner Books, 1998.

Moore, Thomas. *Care of the Soul: A Guide for Cultivating Depth and Sacredness in Everyday Life.* New York: HarperPerennial, 1994.

Peale, Norman Vincent. *Positive Imaging: A Powerful Way to Change Your Life.* New York: Fawcett Columbine, 1982.

Peck, M. Scott. *The Road Less Traveled: A New Psychology of Love, Traditional Values and Spiritual Growth.* New York: Touchstone/Simon & Schuster, 1978.

Nutrition and Recovery

Beasley, Joseph D., and Susan Knightly. *Food For Recovery: The Complete Nutritional Companion for Recovering from Alcoholism, Drug Addiction, and Eating Disorders.* New York: Crown Trade Paperbacks, 1994.

Ketcham, Katherine, and L. Ann Mueller. *Eating Right to Live Sober: A Comprehensive Guide to Alcoholism and Nutrition.* Seattle, WA: Madrona Publishers, 1983.

Mumey, Jack, and Anne S. Hatcher. *Good Food for a Sober Life: A Diet and Nutrition Book for Recovering Alcoholics—and Those Who Love Them.* Chicago: Contemporary Books, 1987.

Oldways Preservation Trust
266 Beacon Street
Boston, MA 02116
(617) 421-5500
E-mail: *oldways@oldwayspt.org*

Oldways is a nonprofit "food issues think tank" dedicated to educating both the general public and health professionals regarding health-conducive food choices. They disseminate various publications, including the "Traditional Healthy Mediterranean Diet Pyramid." They sponsor educational conferences, and their Web site maintains a wealth of "links for wise eating."

Recovery Focused: General

Black, Claudia. *It Will Never Happen to Me: Children of Alcoholics as Youngsters—Adolescents—Adults.* New York: Ballantine Books, 1981.

Chopra, Deepak. *Overcoming Addictions: The Spiritual Solution.* New York: Three Rivers Press, 1997.

Colleran, Carol, and Debra Jay. *Aging and Addiction: Helping Older Adults Overcome Alcohol or Medication Dependence.* Center City, MN: Hazelden, 2000.

Gorski, Terence T. *Passages Through Recovery: An Action Plan for Preventing Relapse.* Center City, MN: Hazelden, 1989.

Gorski, Terence T., and Merlene Miller. *Counseling for Relapse Prevention.* Independence, MO: Herald House/Independence Press, 1982.

Jay, Jeff, and Debra Jay. *Love First: A New Approach to Intervention for Alcoholism & Drug Addiction.* Center City, MN: Hazelden, 2000.

Ketcham, Katherine, and William F. Asbury. *Beyond the Influence: Understanding and Defeating Alcoholism.* New York: Bantam Books, 2000.

Ketcham, Katherine, and Nicholas A. Pace. *Teens Under the Influence: The Truth About Kids, Alcohol, and Other Drugs—How to Recognize the Problem and What to Do About It.* New York: Ballantine Books, 2003.

Marlatt, G. Alan, and Judith R. Gordon, eds. *Relapse Prevention.* New York: Guilford Press, 1985.

Periodicals

Dr. Andrew Weil's Self Healing. A monthly newsletter published by Dr. Andrew Weil, director of the program in Integrative Medicine at the University of Arizona. This is one of my favorite sources of wellness updates. For subscription information call (800) 523-3296 or visit the newsletter Web site at *www.drweilselfhealing.com.*

Natural Health. This semimonthly publication is another of my favorites—chock full of useful tips regarding wellness, self-care and integrative medicine. Includes regular columns by Andrew Weil, Deepak Chopra and other leaders in the field. For subscription information call (515) 246-6952 or visit the Web site at *www.natural healthmag.com.*

Prevention (Rodale Press). This monthly prevention/self-care magazine has been around for decades. Available at your supermarket checkout stand. For subscription information call (800) 813-8070 or visit the Rodale Web site at *www.rodalepress.com.*

Steps for Recovery: The Guide to Clean and Sober Lifestyles. A monthly recovery-focused newspaper, with worldwide circulation, featuring inspirational articles covering all aspects of clean and sober living. Includes a monthly column on wellness and recovery by yours truly. For subscription information call (818) 905-7837.

UC Berkeley Wellness Letter. A monthly newsletter published by the University of California, Berkeley School of Public Health, designed to translate leading-edge research into practical advice for promoting healthy lifestyles. For subscription information call (386) 447-6328 or visit the newsletter Web site at *www.wellnessletter.com.*

Audiocassettes and Videotapes

Emmett E. Miller, M.D.
P.O. Box 6028
Auburn, CA 95604.

Emmett E. Miller, M.D., is the author of *Deep Healing* and creator of the Deep Healing series of CDs, videos and audiocassettes. Dr. Miller is a pioneer in the field of mind/body medicine, and his tapes and videos are designed to facilitate self-healing and complement professional treatment for a wide variety of health concerns. His audiocassettes lead participants through informative and empowering guided imagery experiences, covering the full range of wellness topics. Some of my own favorite titles include *The Serenity Prayer, Change the Channel on Pain* and *Rainbow Butterfly*—my wife's all-time favorite relaxation tape. Dr. Miller also conducts workshops, retreats and professional trainings for health care professionals. To order a current catalog, call (800) 528-2737 or visit Dr. Miller's Web site at *www.DrMiller.com.*

Wellness Centers and Community Resources

Wellness Centers

Deepak Chopra, M.D., Director
Chopra Center for Well-Being at the La Costa Resort and Spa
2013 Costa del Mar Road
Carlsbad, CA 92009
(888) 424-6772
E-mail: *info@chopra.com*
Web site: *www.chopra.com*

The Chopra Center is an educational center, treatment center and spa whose programs embody the philosophical tenets promulgated by Deepak Chopra, which seek to promote optimum health via an integrative approach grounded in the traditions of Ayurvedic medicine. Available services include integrative medical consultations, residential health enhancement programs and Ayurvedic purification/detoxification programs.

Dean Ornish, M.D., Director
The Preventive Medicine Research Institute
900 Bridgeway
Sausalito, CA 94965
(415) 332-2525
Web site: *www.pmri.org*

The Preventive Medicine Research Institute, founded by Dr. Dean Ornish, conducts innovative research, educational and service programs focusing on cardiovascular wellness and other cutting-edge applications of preventive medicine. Through the affiliated Lifestyle Advantage program, locally administered programs centered on Dr. Ornish's principles of reversing heart disease are offered at various sites across the country.

Andrew Weil, M.D., Director
Program in Integrative Medicine
University of Arizona
Tucson, Arizona
Program Web site: *www.integrativemedicine.arizona.edu.*
Dr. Weil's Web site: *www.drweil.com*

The University of Arizona's program in integrative medicine, headed by Dr. Andrew Weil, is designed to promote a healing-oriented approach to medicine that draws upon all therapeutic systems, both conventional and alternative, to form a comprehensive approach to the art and science of medicine. Program offerings include training programs for physicians interested in incorporating integrative medicine into their practices, a physician referral service and an on-site integrative medicine clinic. For information concerning clinic appointments, call 800-524-5928, ext. 500.

Community Resources

Sierra Club
85 Second Street, 2nd Floor
San Francisco, CA 94105
(415) 977-5500

With a membership of over 700,000 and over 460 chapters and groups across the country, the Sierra Club is the nation's largest grassroots environmental organization. In addition to orchestrating public education and lobbying efforts designed to protect the environment, the Sierra Club offers, through its local chapters, a full schedule of hikes, outings and trips to introduce members and guests to the wonders of nature. Joining the Sierra Club is an excellent way to keep in shape by hitting the trails, while meeting other folks in your community who share a common interest in outdoor recreation and preserving our natural heritage of forests, clean air and fresh water. Call or write the central office for further information, or visit the Web site at *www.sierraclub.org.*

Community Colleges

Chances are your local community college offers a wealth of low-cost community service programs dealing with health and wellness.

Through their physical education departments, many community colleges offer low-cost fitness evaluations and physical conditioning programs. Under the umbrella of their community services programs, most community colleges also offer low-cost evening and weekend programs, which include a wide range of wellness topics. Typically, these include courses on stress management, diet and nutrition, other health-related topics, and a wide range of offerings designed to assist participants in fully developing their creative potential. Check your local community college schedule for further details.

Newspapers

Most newspapers feature a weekly health section designed to highlight newsworthy items centered on health and wellness. Items typically featured include:

- Advice columns authored by physicians, nutritionists, fitness trainers, pharmacists, psychotherapists and other health professionals.
- Feature articles highlighting medical breakthroughs, current areas of controversy in health and medicine, profiles of innovative health-related programs serving your community, stories profiling patients who have successfully dealt with challenging health problems, and other health-related topics.
- A calendar of local health-related events, including talks and workshops, health screenings, support group meetings and health fairs.

Check your local newspaper for further details.

Health Plans

Most health plans offer a variety of free-of-charge or low-cost health education programs designed to help their members stay well and healthy. Health education offerings typically include classes focusing on diet and weight loss, smoking cessation, controlling high blood pressure, stress management, and other health-related topics. Most health plans host Web sites offering health care tips and pointers for healthy living. Some of these Web sites feature on-line health risk appraisals, which evaluate your personal profile of health-related behaviors and risk factors, and present customized suggestions concerning steps you can take to bring your health into better balance.

Community Health Fairs

Community health fairs have become popular vehicles for conducting mass health screenings and health education/awareness programs. Screenings are provided either free of charge or at a nominal cost, and typically include blood pressure checks, cholesterol screening, body fat analysis, and screening for glaucoma, diabetes, prostate cancer and other health conditions. You can acquire a wealth of useful information by investing an afternoon attending a health fair in your community. Health fairs are generally offered on weekends at community college campuses, hospitals and other community sites. As part of their employee benefit programs, many large companies conduct annual health fairs for their employees.

Wellness-Oriented Web Sites

You can obtain a wealth of information on just about any health-related subject simply by doing an on-line search. Just remember that these on-line informational resources vary widely in terms of the accuracy and credibility of information provided. The following is a sampling of selected health-related Web sites that are both credible and highly informative.

Healthfinder
www.healthfinder.gov

Healthfinder is an extremely informative Web site maintained by the Office of Disease Prevention and Health Promotion of the U.S. Department of Health and Human Services, with support from the National Health Information Center and other federal agencies. Healthfinder features links to more than 1,800 health-related organizations. Web site content includes:

- an extensive on-line health library:
- a "just for you" section, featuring selected health topics organized for men and women, for people of all ages, by race and ethnicity, and for parents, caregivers, health professionals and others; and
- an extensive on-line database of information covering a wide range of health-related topics, including doctors, dentists and hospitals, health insurance, prescription drugs, health fraud, Medicare, Medicaid, and medical privacy.

Helios Health
www.helioshealth.com

The Helios Health Web site features an abundant base of information on a wide range of health-related topics. Although the Web site is sponsored by participating pharmaceutical companies and other health product vendors, their articles provide an objective, well-balanced perspective. Helios provides free-of-charge e-stations in the waiting rooms of general practitioners and women's health practices across the country, enabling patients to access valuable health-related information on-line while waiting to see their doctors.

MedLine Plus
www.medlineplus.gov

MedLine Plus is jointly sponsored by the National Library of Medicine and the National Institutes of Health. This Web site provides a wealth of reliable health information from the world's largest medical library, the National Library of Medicine. This site is a favorite with consumers and health professionals alike. Content includes:

- A data base featuring over 600 health-related topics.
- Information on prescriptions and over-the-counter drugs.
- An illustrated medical encyclopedia and medical dictionary.
- Health-related news updates.
- Directories of doctors, dentists, hospitals, consumer health libraries and more.

WedMD Health
www.webmd.com

WebMD is a leading provider of software for medical practices, and its WebMD Health site is a leading provider of on-line information and educational services for both physicians and consumers. The Web site features an extensive database on diseases and conditions, directories of doctors and other health care providers, access to on-line chat groups, and an extensive health and wellness section. If you enjoy newsletters, the WebMD Health site enables you to subscribe to close to thirty e-health newsletters featuring various health and wellness topics.

Web Sites Hosted by Voluntary Health Associations

The major voluntary health associations maintain extensive Web sites designed to educate and inform users regarding their program focuses. The following is a list of several of the larger voluntary associations and their Web addresses.

American Cancer Society
www.cancer.org

American Heart Association
www.americanheart.org

American Lung Association
www.lungusa.org

Web site includes on-site access to the American Lung Association's "Freedom from Smoking" smoking cessation program.

Recovery-Focused Resources

This section highlights selected recovery-focused resources of potential interest to both the general public and alcoholism/drug abuse treatment professionals.

Center for Applied Sciences (CENAPS)
Terence T. Gorski, Director
6147 Deltona Boulevard
Spring Hill, Florida 34606
(352) 596-8000
E-mail: *info@enaps.com*
Web site: *www.tgorski.com*

CENAPS is an addictions training and consulting firm founded by Terence T. Gorski. CENAPS is committed to providing advanced clinical skills-training for addictions professionals, with special emphasis on preventing relapse, early relapse intervention, and assisting recovering alcoholics and addicts in lifetime growth and learning throughout the recovery process.

Specific program focuses include clinical skills-training for treatment providers, consultation services for managed care programs and treatment professionals, and education and training products, including audio and video assisted consultation packets and recovery guides. Training workshops are offered at sites throughout the country. For a current schedule consult Terry Gorski's Clinical Development Web site at *www.tgorski.com*

Employee Assistance Professionals Association
2101 Wilson Boulevard, Suite 500
Arlington, VA 22201-3062
(703) 387-1000
Web site: *www.eapassn.org*

The Employee Assistance Professionals Association (EAPA) is dedicated to advancing professional development of employee assistance professionals throughout the world. With over one hundred chapters worldwide, EAPA regularly hosts continuing education programs that are widely attended by employee assistance professionals, as well as by addictions treatment professionals and mental health professionals working with clients suffering from addictive disorders. Many of these programs focus on stress management and other topics relating to wellness and recovery. EAPA publishes a bimonthly professional journal, *EAPA Exchange,* and offers a certification program for employee assistance professionals through the affiliated Employee Assistance Certification Commission.

Love First: Intervention for Alcoholism and Drug Addiction

Jeff Jay and Debra Jay (intervention specialists based in Grosse Pointe Farms, Michigan)

(313) 882-6921

Web site: *www.lovefirst.net*

Jeff and Debra Jay are coauthors of *Love First: A New Approach to Intervention for Alcoholism & Drug Addiction*. Their groundbreaking book outlines an innovative approach to motivating alcoholics and addicts to enter treatment, which is based on confronting the alcoholic/addict with love, in contrast to other approaches to intervention that tend to rely more heavily on coercive efforts. According to Jeff and Debra, "When the role of love takes center stage during an intervention, most families never have to resort to using tough love." The Jays maintain a national intervention practice and are available to provide structured intervention services, training programs and consultations for families and treatment professionals throughout the country.

National Association of Alcoholism and Drug Abuse Counselors

901 N. Washington Street, Suite 600

Alexandria, VA 22314

(800) 548-0497

Web site: *www.naadac.org*

The National Association of Alcoholism and Drug Abuse Counselors (NAADAC) is the premier global organization representing addictions professionals who are dedicated to enhancing the health and recovery of individuals, families and communities. NAADAC's organizational structure includes close to 14,000 members and 47 state affiliates. NAADAC promotes excellence in care via its national certification program for addictions counselors, as well as by providing extensive educational and clinical training services through both the national organization and its state affiliates, and through its bimonthly publication *Counselor: The Magazine for Addiction Professionals*.

Nicotine Anonymous

World Services

419 Main Street, PMB #370

Huntington Beach, CA 92648

(415) 750-0328

Web site: *www.nicotine-anonymous.org*

Nicotine Anonymous (NicA) is a 12-step program dedicated to helping men and women live nicotine-free lives. Their Web site provides a worldwide directory of NicA meetings, an order form for NicA publications, and a calendar of NicA-sponsored conferences and retreats.

References

Introduction

Beattie, Melody. *Codependent No More.* Center City, MN: Hazelden, 1992.

Chapter 1: Wellness: The Missing Dimension in Recovery

Falkowski, Carol. *Dangerous Drugs: An Easy-to-Use Reference for Parents and Professionals.* Center City, MN: Hazelden, 2000.

Glasser, William. *Positive Addiction.* New York: Harper & Row, 1976.

Kuhn, Cynthia, Scott Swartzwelder, and Wilkin Wilson. *Buzzed: The Straight Facts About the Most Used and Abused Drugs From Alcohol to Ecstasy.* New York: W.W. Norton & Co., 2003.

Williams, G.D., B. F. Grant, T. C. Harford, and J. Noble. "Epidemiological Bulletin No. 23: Population Projections Using DSM-III Criteria: Alcohol Abuse and Dependence, 1990–2000." *Alcohol Health & Research World* 13, no. 4 (1989): 366–370.

Chapter 2: Importance of Wellness to Early Recovery and Relapse Prevention

Chartier, Brent. "Exxon's 'Never-Ever' Policy on Trial." *EAP Digest* (Winter 2000): 18–25.

Dorsman, Jerry. *How to Quit Drugs for Good: A Complete Self-Help Guide.* Roseville, CA: Prima Publishing, 1998.

Gallant, Donald M. *Alcoholism: A Guide to Diagnosis, Intervention, and Treatment.* New York: W. W. Norton & Co., 1987.

Gelderloos, Paul, et al. "Effectiveness of the Transcendental Meditation Program in Preventing and Treating Substance Misuse: A Review." *The International Journal of the Addictions* 26, no. 3 (1991): 293–325.

Glasser, William. *Positive Addiction.* New York: Harper & Row, 1976.

Gorski, Terence T. *Passages Through Recovery: An Action Plan for Preventing Relapse.* Center City, MN: Hazelden, 1989.

———. Interview conducted on March 22, 2004.

Gorski, Terence T., and Merlene Miller. *Counseling for Relapse Prevention.* Independence, MO: Herald House/Independence Press, 1982.

L. R. "Chronic Relapse." *Steps for Recovery,* September 2003.

Marlatt, G. Alan, and Judith Gordon, eds. *Relapse Prevention: Maintenance Strategies in the Treatment of Addictive Behaviors.* New York: Guilford Press, 1985.

National Institute on Alcohol Abuse and Alcoholism. "Relapse and Craving." *Alcohol Alert* 6 (1989).

Newport, John. "The Wellness-Recovery Connection." *EAP Digest* (Winter 2000): 28–30.

Sinyor, David, et al. "The Role of a Physical Fitness Program in Treatment of Alcoholism." *Journal of Studies on Alcohol* 43, no. 3 (1982): 380–386.

Chapter 3: Claiming Your Birthright to Optimal Health

Ardell, Donald B. *High Level Wellness: An Alternative to Doctors, Drugs and Disease.* Berkeley, CA: Ten Speed Press, 1986.

"CDC's Battle of the Bulge: Escalating Obesity in U.S." *Los Angeles Times* (October 4, 2000).

"HealthierUS: The President's Health and Fitness Initiative." White House Web site: *www.whitehouse.gov/infocus/fitness,* 2003.

Hedley, Allison A., et al. "Prevalence of Overweight and Obesity Among US Children, Adolescents, and Adults, 1999–2002." *Journal of the American Medical Association* 291, no. 23 (2004): 2847–2850.

Newport, John. "Wellness: It's A Way of Life." *Health Focus,* General Med Health Plan (Fall 1985): 5.

———. "Only Prevention Can Preserve Us." *Health Care Business* (March-April 2000): 104.

———. "The Wellness, Recovery Connection." *EAP Digest* (Winter 2000): 28–30.

Pelletier, Kenneth R. *Longevity: Fulfilling Our Biological Potential.* New York: Delta/ Seymour Lawrence, 1981.

"Surgeon General Takes Stern Stance on Obesity." *Los Angeles Times* (December 14, 2001).

Travis, John W., and Regina Sara Ryan. *Wellness Workbook.* Berkeley, CA: Ten Speed Press, 2004.

Weil, Andrew. "Childhood Obesity: A Weighty Issue." *Dr. Andrew Weil's Self Healing,* October 2002.

Chapter 4: Nutritional Hazards Associated With Alcoholism and Drug Addiction

American Cancer Society 1996 Advisory Committee on Diet, Nutrition and Cancer Prevention. "Guidelines on Diet, Nutrition, and Cancer Prevention: Reducing the Risk of Cancer with Healthy Food Choices and Physical Activity." *CA—A Cancer Journal for Clinicians* 46, no. 6 (1996): 325–341.

American Dietetic Association. "Position of the American Dietetic Association: Nutrition Intervention in Treatment and Recovery from Chemical Dependency." *Journal of the American Dietetic Association* 90, no. 9 (1990): 1274–1277.

American Obesity Association. "Obesity in the U.S." American Obesity Association Web site: *www.obesity.org.*

Beasley, Joseph D., and Susan Knightly. *Food For Recovery: The Complete Nutritional Companion for Recovering from Alcoholism, Drug Addiction and Eating Disorders.* New York: Crown Trade Paperbacks, 1994.

"CDC's Battle of the Bulge: Escalating Obesity in U.S." *Los Angeles Times* (October 4, 2000).

"Doctors Worry as 3-Year-Olds Show Fatty Deposits in Aorta." *Associated Press* (July 8, 2002).

Gallant, Donald M. *Alcoholism: A Guide to Diagnosis, Intervention, and Treatment.* New York: W. W. Norton & Co, 1987.

Gorski, Terence T. (1989). *Passages Through Recovery: An Action Plan for Preventing Relapse.* Center City, MN: Hazelden.

Hedley, Allison A., et al. "Prevalence of Overweight and Obesity Among US Children, Adolescents, and Adults, 1999–2002." *Journal of the American Medical Association* 291, no. 23 (2004): 2847–2850.

Ketcham, Katherine, and L. Ann Mueller. *Eating Right to Live Sober: A Comprehensive Guide to Alcoholism and Nutrition.* Seattle, WA: Madrona Publishers, 1983.

"Lifestyle Called Key to Averting Diabetes." *Los Angeles Times* (August 10, 2001).

"Medical System Losing Battle with Severe Obesity." *Los Angeles Daily News* (October 14, 2003).

Mumey, Jack, and Anne S. Hatcher. *Good Food for a Sober Life: A Diet and Nutrition Book for Recovering Alcoholics—and Those Who Love Them.* Chicago: Contemporary Books, 1987.

National Institute on Alcohol Abuse and Alcoholism. "Alcohol and Nutrition." *Alcohol Alert 22* (1993).

"Obesity Has More Links to Cancer." *Los Angeles Times* (April 24, 2003).

"Politicians Chew on Weight Issue." *Associated Press* (August 25, 2003).

"Study: Obesity at Young Age is Deadly, Too." *Associated Press* (January 8, 2003).

"Surgeon General Takes Stern Stance on Obesity." *Los Angeles Times* (December 14, 2001).

Williams, Roger J. *The Prevention of Alcoholism Through Nutrition.* New York: Bantam Books, 1971.

Chapter 5: Your Nutritional Foundation For Recovery

American Dietetic Association. "Position of the American Dietetic Association: Nutrition Intervention in Treatment and Recovery from Chemical Dependency." *Journal of the American Dietetic Association* 90, no. 9 (1990): 1274–1277.

Ardell, Donald B. *High Level Wellness: An Alternative to Doctors, Drugs and Disease.* Berkeley, CA: Ten Speed Press, 1986.

Beasley, Joseph D. and Susan Knightly. *Food For Recovery: The Complete Nutritional Companion for Recovering from Alcoholism, Drug Addiction and Eating Disorders.* New York: Crown Trade Paperbacks, 1994.

Dorsman, Jerry. *How to Quit Drugs for Good: A Complete Self-Help Guide.* Roseville, CA: Prima Publishing, 1998.

"Global Health Panel Expresses Concerns on Fried Food Risks." *Los Angeles Times* (June 28, 2002).

"HealthierUS: The President's Health and Fitness Initiative—The President's Recommendations for Improving Nutrition." White House Web site: *www.white house.gov/infocus/fitness*, 2003.

"Heart-Healthy Omega-3 May be Good for Your Brain." *Washington Post* Service (September, 10, 2003).

Katzen, Molly. "Diet? Don't Buy It." *Body and Soul* (Winter 2003): 32.

Ketcham, Katherine, and William F. Asbury. *Beyond the Influence: Understanding and Defeating Alcoholism.* New York: Bantam Books, 2000.

Ketcham, Katherine, and L. Ann Mueller. *Eating Right to Live Sober: A Comprehensive Guide to Alcoholism and Nutrition.* Seattle, WA: Madrona Publishers, 1983.

Moore Lappé. Frances. *Diet for a Small Planet.* New York: Ballantine Books, 1992.

Lewis, Alan E. *Nutrition in Recovery Handbook: Nutritional Support for Addiction Recovery.* Clayton, CA: Pacific Biologic, 2001.

Mumey, Jack, and Anne S. Hatcher. *Good Food for a Sober Life: A Diet and Nutrition Book for Recovering Alcoholics—and Those Who Love Them.* Chicago: Contemporary Books, 1987.

Oldways Preservation and Exchange Trust. "The Mediterranean Diet Pyramid." Oldways Web site: *www.oldwayspt.org/pyramids/med/*

Pelletier, Kenneth R. *Longevity: Fulfilling Our Biological Potential.* New York: Delta/Seymour Lawrence, 1981.

"Serve Up the Veggies, Not Fad Diets." *Los Angeles Times* (September 23, 2002).

"The Food Pyramid: Does It Miss the Point?" *Los Angeles Times* (September 1, 2000).

"The Food Guide Pyramid: Your Personal Guide to Healthful Eating." International Food Information Council Foundation, U.S. Department of Agriculture and Food Marketing Institute (undated).

Weil, Andrew. *Eating Well for Optimum Health.* New York: Alfred A. Knopf, 2000.

———. "Changing Times for Organic Foods." *Dr. Andrew Weil's Self Healing,* August 2002.

———. "Remodeling the Food Pyramid." *Dr. Andrew Weil's Weekly Wellness Bulletin* (September 23, 2003).

Williams, Roger J. *The Prevention of Alcoholism Through Nutrition.* New York: Bantam Books, 1971.

Witt, Kara F. "Snacking While Working: The New Occupational Health Hazard?" *EAPA Exchange,* July/August 2001.

Chapter 6: Physical Exercise: Fitness and Recovery

American College of Sports Medicine. "Americans Urged to Embrace Current Physical Activity Guidelines to Live Longer, Healthier Lives." Press release, April 11, 2003.

American College of Sports Medicine. "Short Brisk Walks Help Fitness, Heart Health and Mood." Press release, September 2000.

"Americans Fall Behind on Exercise." Associated Press (August 15, 2003).

Centers for Disease Control and Prevention. "Physical Activity and Public Health— A Recommendation from the Centers for Disease Control and Prevention and the American College of Sports Medicine." *Journal of the American Medical Association* 273, no. 5 (1995): 402–407.

Gorski, Terence T. *Passages Through Recovery: An Action Plan for Preventing Relapse.* Center City, MN: Hazelden, 1989.

"HealthierUS: The President's Health and Fitness Initiative—The President's Recommendations for Improving Physical Fitness." White House Web site: *www.whitehouse.gov/infocus/fitness*, 2003.

Institute of Medicine. "Dietary Reference Intakes for Energy, Carbohydrate, Fiber, Fat, Fatty Acids, Cholesterol, Protein, and Amino Acids." Washington, D.C.: The National Academies Press, 2002.

Los Angeles County Department of Health Services. "L.A. Health—Physical Activity Among Adults in Los Angeles County." November 2000.

Matthews, Charles E., et al. "Moderate to Vigorous Physical Activity and Risk of Upper-Respiratory Tract Infection." *Medicine & Science in Sports & Exercise,* American College of Sports Medicine (2002): 1242–1248.

Newport, John. *Influence of a Wellness-Oriented Lifestyle on Successfulness of Recovery from Chemical Dependency.* Doctoral dissertation: California Coast University, Santa Ana, CA, 1998.

Palmer, James, Nicholas Vacc, and John Epstein. "Adult Inpatient Alcoholics: Physical Exercise as a Treatment Intervention." *Journal of Studies on Alcohol* 49, no. 5 (1988): 418–421.

Sinyor, David, Tom Brown, Loraine Rostant, and Peter Seraganian. "The Role of a Physical Fitness Program in the Treatment of Alcoholism." *Journal of Studies on Alcohol* 43, no. 3 (1982): 380–386.

Weil, Andrew. "Walking for Wellness." *Dr. Andrew Weil's Self Healing* (April 1998): 8.

"Work Up to Better Health." *Los Angeles Times* (September 16, 2002).

Chapter 7: Stress Management and Meditation

Benson, Herbert. *Timeless Healing.* New York: Scribner, 1996.

Braiken, Harriet B. *The September 11 Syndrome: Anxious Days and Sleepless Nights—Seven Steps to Getting A Grip in Uncertain Times.* New York: McGraw-Hill, 2002.

Brown, Sandra A., Michael Irwin, and Marc A. Schukit. "Changes in Anxiety Among Abstinent Male Alcoholics." *Journal of Studies on Alcohol* 52, no. 1 (1991): 55.

Cohen, S., D. A. Tyrrell, and A. P. Smith. "Psychological Stress and Susceptibility to the Common Cold." *New England Journal of Medicine* 325 (1991): 606–612.

Elliott, Robert S.. *From Stress to Strength.* New York: Bantam Books, 1994.

"Emotional Stress Poses More Risk." Copley News Service, September, 25, 2002.

Gelderloos, Paul, Kenneth G. Walton, David W. Orme-Johnson, and Charles N. Alexander. "Effectiveness of the Transcendental Meditation Program in Preventing and Treating Substance Misuse: A Review." *The International Journal of the Addictions* 26, no. 3 (1991): 293–325.

Giuliani, Rudolph W. *Leadership.* New York: Miramax Books, 2002.

Gorski, Terence T. *Passages Through Recovery: An Action Plan for Preventing Relapse.* Center City, MN: Hazelden, 1989.

Gorski, Terence T. "Dawning of A New Day: Addiction Recovery in the Age of Terrorism." Gorski—CENAPS Web site: *www.tgorski.com*, December 20, 2001.

Hafen, Brent Q., Keith J. Karren, Kathryn J. Frandsen and N. Lee Smith. *Mind/Body Health.* Needham Heights, MA: Allyn & Bacon, 1996.

"Is Trauma Debriefing Worse Than Letting Victims Heal Naturally?" *Wall Street Journal* (September 12, 2003).

Mumey, Jack, and Anne S. Hatcher. *Good Food for a Sober Life.* Chicago: Contemporary Books, 1987.

Newport, John (1998). *Influence of a Wellness-Oriented Lifestyle on Successfulness of Recovery from Chemical Dependency.* Doctoral Dissertation: California Coast University, Santa Ana, CA, 1998.

———. "The Wellness-Recovery Connection." *EAP Digest* (Winter 2000): 28–30.

———. "A Stress Management Tool That Really Works." *Steps for Recovery* (February 2003).

———. "Add This to Your Stress Management Tool Kit." *Steps for Recovery* (January 2004).

Reich, Peter. "How Much Does Stress Contribute to Cardiovascular Disease?" *Journal of Cardiovascular Medicine* (July 1983): 825–831.

Ridgewood, Sonja Steptoe. "Ready, Set, Relax!—Fed Up With the Fast Track, People Are Banding Together to Find Ways to Slow Things Down." *Time* (October 27, 2003): 38–39, 1.

Rosenman, Ray H., et al. "Coronary Heart Disease in the Western Collaborative Group Study: Final Follow-up Experience of 8 1/2 Years." *Journal of the American Medical Association* 233, no. 8 (1975): 872–877.

Seward, Brian Luke. *Stressed Is Desserts Spelled Backward.* New York: Barnes & Noble Books, 1999.

Tucker, Larry A., Galen E. Cole, and Glenn M. Friedman. "Stress and Serum Cholesterol: A Study of 7,000 Adult Males." *Health Values* 2, no. 3 (1987): 34–39.

Chapter 8: Developing a Strong Social Support System

Anand, Margo. *The Art of Sexual Ecstasy: The Path of Sacred Sexuality for Western Lovers.* New York: Jeremy P. Tarcher/Putnam, 1989.

Beattie, Melody. *Codependent No More.* Center City, MN: Hazelden, 1992.

Black, Claudia. *It Will Never Happen to Me: Adult Children of Alcoholics As Youngsters—Adolescents—Adults.* New York: Ballantine, 1981.

Bradshaw, John. *Bradshaw On: The Family—A New Way of Creating Solid Self-Esteem.* Deerfield Beach, FL: Health Communications, Inc., 1996.

Bromet, Evelyn, and Rudolf Moss. "Sex and Marital Status in Relation to the Characteristics of Alcoholics." *Journal of Studies on Alcohol* 37, no. 9 (1976): 1302–1312.

Brown, Sandra A., et al. "Stress, Vulnerability and Adult Alcohol Relapse." *Journal of Studies on Alcohol* 56 (1995): 538–545.

Gorski, Terence T. *Passages Through Recovery: An Action Plan for Preventing Relapse.* Center City, MN: Hazelden, 1989.

Hafen, Brent Q., Keith J. Karren, Kathryn J. Frandsen, and N. Lee Smith. *Mind/Body Health.* Boston: Allyn and Bacon, 1996.

Heisel, J. Stephen, Steven E. Locke, Linda J. Kraus, and Michael R. Williams. "Natural Killer Cell Activity and MMPI Scores of a Cohort of College Students." *American Journal of Psychiatry* 143 (1986): 1382–1386.

Living Sober. New York: Alcoholics Anonymous World Services, 1988.

Locke, Steven, and Douglas Colligan. *The Healer Within.* New York: E.P. Dutton, 1986.

Lynch, James. S. *The Broken Heart: The Medical Consequences of Loneliness.* New York: Basic Books, 1977.

"Marriage and Wellness Linked." *Deseret News* (November 15: 1988): 4A.

Newport, John. *Influence of a Wellness-Oriented Lifestyle on Successfulness of Recovery from Chemical Dependency.* Doctoral Dissertation: California Coast University, Santa Ana, CA, 1998.

———. "The Wellness-Recovery Connection." *EAP Digest,* Winter 2000.

———. "Advance Warning—Coping With the Holiday Crazies." *Steps for Recovery* (November 2002).

———. "Breaking the Cycle of Depression (Part 1)." *Steps for Recovery* (October 2003).

Rosenthal, Saul H. *Sex Over 40.* New York: Jeremy P. Tarcher/Putnam, 1999.

Sarason, Barbara R., Irwin G. Sarason, and Gregory R. Peirce. *Social Support: An Interactive View.* New York: John Wiley & Sons, 1990.

"Surviving a Heart Attack: Emotional Support Is Key." *Mental Medicine Update 2* (Spring 1993).

Syme, S. Leonard. "Coronary Artery Disease: A Sociocultural Perspective." *Circulation 76* (1987): Supplement I.

Tooley, Jo Ann, and Lynn Y. Anderson. "Living Is Risky." *U.S. News and World Report* (January 25, 1988).

Turkington, Carol. "Have You Hugged Your Immune System Today?" *Self* (October 1988).

U.S. Department of Health, Education and Welfare, Public Health Service. *Healthy People: The Surgeon General's Report on Health Promotion and Disease Prevention.* DHEW (PHS) Publication No. 79–55071. Washington, D.C.: U.S. Government Printing Office, 1979.

Chapter 9: Central Purpose, Spirituality and Life Satisfaction

Ash, Mel. *The Zen of Recovery.* New York: Jeremy P. Tarcher/Putnam, 1992.

Chopra, Deepak. *The Seven Spiritual Laws of Success.* San Rafael, CA: Amber-Allen Publishing/New World Library, 1994.

Dalai Lama. *Ethics for the New Millennium.* New York: Riverhead Books, 1999.

Farmer, Steven D. *Sacred Ceremony: How to Create Ceremonies for Healing, Transitions, and Celebrations.* Carlsbad, CA: Hay House, 2002.

Fox, Emmett. *The Lord's Prayer: An Interpretation.* Marina del Rey, CA: De Vorrs & Co., 1963.

Ketcham, Katherine, and William F. Asbury. *Beyond the Influence: Understanding and Defeating Alcoholism.* New York: Bantam Books, 2000.

Marlatt, G. Alan, and Judith Gordon, Judith, eds. *Relapse Prevention: Maintenance Strategies in the Treatment of Addictive Behaviors.* New York: Guilford Press, 1985.

Millman, Dan. *Everyday Enlightenment: The Twelve Gateways to Personal Growth.* New York: Warner Books, 1988.

Moore, Thomas. *Care of the Soul: A Guide for Cultivating Depth and Sacredness in Everyday Life.* New York: Harper Perennial, 1992.

Newport, John. "Central Purpose: The Royal Road to Health & Longevity." *Steps for Recovery* (October 2002).

Peck, M. Scott. *The Road Less Traveled.* New York: Simon & Schuster, 1978.

"Searching for a Happiness Strategy." *Los Angeles Times* (December 9, 2003).

Thich Nhat Hanh. *The Wisdom of Thich Nhat Hanh: The Miracle of Mindfulness, Being Peace, The Sun My Heart, Touching Peace.* New York: One Spirit, 2000.

Twelve Steps and Twelve Traditions. New York: Alcoholics Anonymous World Services, 1952; 2003 (38th Printing).

Zukav, Gary. *The Seat of the Soul.* New York: Fireside/Simon & Schuster, 1989.

Chapter 10: Conquering Nicotine Addiction

American Cancer Society. "The Choice is Smoking or Health." American Cancer Society Web site: *www.cancer.org*, 2004.

Bobo, Janet K. "Nicotine Dependence and Alcoholism Epidemiology and Treatment." *Journal of Psychoactive Drugs* 21 (1989): 323–329.

Bobo, Janet K., Robert F. Schilling, Lewayne D. Gilchrist, and Steven Paul Schinke. "The Double Triumph: Sustained Sobriety and Successful Cigarette Smoking Cessation." *Journal of Substance Abuse Treatment* 3 (1986): 21–25.

"California Called Model on Tobacco." *Los Angeles Times* (February 9, 2001).

Centers for Disease Control. "Annual Smoking—Attributable Mortality, Years of Potential Life Lost, and Economic Costs—United States, 1995–1999." MMWR 51 (2002): 300–303.

County of Los Angeles, Department of Health Services, Public Health. "Adult Smoking." December 2003.

Di Franza, Joseph R., and Mary P. Guerrera. "Alcoholism and Smoking." *Journal of Studies on Alcohol* 51, no. 2 (1990): 130–135.

Falkowski, Carol L. "Addressing Nicotine Addiction—When is the "Right Time?" *Counselor* (August 2003): 12–17.

Gulliver, Suzy Bird, et al. (1995). "Interrelationship of Smoking and Alcohol Dependence: Use and Urges to Use." *Journal of Studies on Alcohol* 56 (1995): 202–206.

National Cancer Institute (1999). "Health Effects of Exposure to Environmental Tobacco Smoke: The Report of the California Environmental Protection Agency." Smoking and Tobacco Control Monograph No. 10. U.S. Department of Health and Human Services, Public Health Service, National Institutes of Health, National Cancer Institute (1999): NIH Publication 99–4645.

National Institute on Alcohol Abuse and Alcoholism. "Alcohol and Tobacco." *Alcohol Alert* 39 (1998).

National Institute of Diabetes and Digestive and Kidney Diseases. "You Can Control Your Weight as You Quit Smoking." NIH Publication (2003): 03–4159.

National Institute on Drug Abuse (NIDA). "NIDA Info Facts: Cigarettes and Other Nicotine Products." NIDA Web site: *www.nida.nih.gov/infofax/tobacco,* 2003.

Newport, John. "The Wellness-Recovery Connection." *EAP Digest* (Winter 2000): 28–30.

"Nicotine Patch Works for Long-Time Sober Smokers." *Wellness Junction Professional Update.* Health Resources Publishing, November 19, 2003.

Sees, Karen Lea, and H. Westley Clark. "When to Begin Smoking Cessation in Substance Abusers." *Journal of Substance Abuse Treatment* 10 (1993): 189–195.

"The Phones Light Up, Not the Callers." *Los Angeles Times* (October 7, 2002).

"The Right Diet for Quitting." *Los Angeles Times* (January 6, 2003).

U.S. Department of Health and Human Services. *The Health Consequences of Smoking: A Report of the Surgeon General—2004.* Washington, D.C.: U.S. Government Printing Office.

Wallace, J. Editorial: "Smoke Gets in Our Eyes: Professional Denial of Smoking." *Journal of Substance Abuse Treatment* 3 (1986): 67–68.

Wise, R.A. "The Neurobiology of Craving: Implications for Understanding and Treatment of Addiction." *Journal of Abnormal Psychology* 97 (1988): 118–132.

Chapter 11: Conducting Your Personal Wellness Assessment

American Heart Association. "Blood Pressure Levels." American Heart Association Web site: *www.americanheart.org,* 2003.

American Heart Association. "Cholesterol Levels." American Heart Association Web site: *www.americanheart.org,* 2003.

Chobinian, Aram V., et al. "The Seventh Report of the Joint National Committee on Prevention, Detection, Evaluation, and Treatment of High Blood Pressure." *Journal of the American Medical Association* 289, no. 19 (2003): 2560.

"Feeling the Pressure." Copley News Service (December 1, 2003).

National Heart, Lung, and Blood Institute. "Calculate Your Body Mass Index." National Heart, Lung, and Blood Institute Web site: *www.nhlbisupport.com/bmi,* 2003.

"New Guide Details 'Prehypertension' Perils." *Los Angeles Times* (May 15, 2003).

"Obesity Greatly Increases Risk of Heart Failure, Study Finds." *The Olympian* (August 2, 2002).

Ornish, Dean. *Dr. Dean Ornish's Program for Reversing Heart Disease.* New York: Ballantine Books, 1990.

"Report Raises Blood Pressure Concerns." Associated Press (May 15, 2003).

Chapter 12: Action Planning for Wellness: Getting Started, Monitoring Your Progress and Following Through

Dallek, Robert. "The Medical Ordeals of JFK." *The Atlantic Monthly* (December 2002): 49–61.

Chapter 13: Making Optimal Use of Health Care Resources

"A Dose of Herbal Reform." *Los Angeles Times* (April 10, 2002).

"Alternative Addiction Treatment." *Counselor: The Magazine for Addiction Professionals* 2, no. 5 (October 2001) Special Edition.

Ang-Lee, Michael K., Jonathan Moss, and Chun-Su Yuan. "Herbal Medicine and Preoperative Care." *Journal of the American Medical Association* 286 (2001): 208–216.

Astin, J.A. (1998) "Why Patients Use Alternative Medicine: Results of a Nationwide Study." *Journal of the American Medical Association* 279 (1998): 1548–1553.

Beasley, Joseph D. and Susan Knightly. *Food for Recovery: The Complete Nutritional Companion for Recovering from Alcoholism, Drug Addiction, and Eating Disorders.* New York: Crown Trade Paperbacks, 1994.

Eisenberg, D.M., et al. "Unconventional Medicine in the United States—Prevalence, Costs and Patterns of Use." *New England Journal of Medicine* 328 (1993): 246–252.

"Ephedra Industry Insists Herb is Safe." *Los Angeles Times* (February 21, 2003).

Fong, Tony. "Looking For A Slowdown—CMS Sees Spending Growth Slowed, But Not All See It." *Modern Healthcare* 8 (February 16, 2004).

Gaudet, Tracy W. "Integrative Medicine: The Evolution of a New Approach to Medicine and Medical Education." *Integrative Medicine* 1, no. 2 (1988): 67–73.

"Get Ephedra Off the Shelves." *Los Angeles Times* (February 21, 2003).

"Health Costs to Outpace Economy." Associated Press (February 7, 2003).

"Herb Stimulant Probed." Associated Press (February 20, 2003).

Ketcham, Katherine, and L. Ann Mueller. *Eating Right to Live Sober: A Comprehensive Guide to Alcoholism and Nutrition.* Seattle: Madrona Publishers, 1983.

Newport, John. "Only Prevention Can Preserve Us: Paying Lip Service to Health Enhancement, Maintenance and Prevention is Not Enough." *Healthcare Business* 104 (March/April 2000).

——. "How to Make Your Health Plan Work For You." *Steps for Recovery* (June 2001).

——. "Take Charge of Your Health." *Steps for Recovery* (November 2001).

"Report Says Health Spending Jump is Biggest in a Decade." Associated Press (January 8, 2003).

"The Diet-Supplement Fiasco." *Los Angeles Times* (December 31, 2003).

Theodosakis, Jason and David Feinberg. *Don't Let Your HMO Kill You.* New York: Routledge, 2000.

"U.S. Intends to Ban Diet Aid Ephedra." *Los Angeles Times* (December 31, 2003).

About the Author

J ohn Newport is a freelance writer and wellness counselor based in Santa Ana, California. He holds combined doctorates in psychology and public health, and he is a certified employee assistance professional.

Dr. Newport is uniquely qualified as an authority on the wellness-recovery connection. As a professor in the early 1980s, he pioneered one of the first university-level courses focusing on holistic health and high-level wellness. He has also served as wellness coordinator for a major California HMO, as chemical dependency program development and marketing specialist with a major psychiatric chain, and as designer of one of California's first HMO-based benefits packages focusing on alcohol and drug rehabilitation.

His doctoral dissertation in psychology focused on exploring the powerful connection between a wellness-oriented lifestyle and successful recovery from chemical dependency, and forms the basis for many of the concepts presented in *The Wellness-Recovery Connection*. Dr. Newport is a prolific writer with over one hundred published articles, and he writes a monthly column on wellness and recovery for *Steps for Recovery*, a periodical with a worldwide circulation of 35,000.

Dr. Newport travels across the country, presenting talks and workshops on wellness and recovery at national and regional conferences, as well as for treatment center staffs and clients. As a wellness counselor, he is available to conduct individual wellness consultations both in his home base in Southern California and on the road. He lives in Southern California with his wife, Ann, and his hobbies include hiking in the desert and mountains, folk singing, and contemporary jazz.

Share Your Journeys in Wellness and Recovery

I hope you have enjoyed *The Wellness-Recovery Connection* and that you will be inspired to pursue your own pathway to optimal health following the guidelines presented in this book. As you conduct your journey in wellness and recovery, I would be interested in hearing from you regarding your progress.

I am presently in the process of writing a sequel to *The Wellness-Recovery Connection,* to be entitled *Journeys in Wellness and Recovery.* I am planning to base this book on firsthand accounts provided by recovering alcoholics/addicts and their family members concerning milestones that readers have accomplished in integrating a wellness-oriented lifestyle into their recovery programs. Setbacks and comebacks encountered along the way will also be featured. I am particularly interested in learning about readers' experiences in overcoming obstacles to wellness and recovery posed by illnesses and other challenging circumstances. In keeping with 12-step traditions, your anonymity will be fully preserved in any treatment dealing with your experience, unless you grant me your express permission to disclose your identity. If you have an experience in wellness and recovery that you would like to share, please send it to me at:

John Newport, Ph.D.
The Wellness-Recovery Connection
Web site: *www.wellnessandrecovery.com*

Please be sure to include information about how I can get in touch with you for follow-up purposes.

Dr. John Newport's Wellness and Recovery Web Site

For further information on wellness and recovery, visit Dr. Newport's Wellness and Recovery Web site at *www.wellnessand recovery.com*. This Web site features periodic updates on topics relating to wellness and recovery, together with a calendar of talks, book signings and workshops conducted by Dr. Newport.

Code #0669 • Hardcover • $19.95

Following in the groundbreaking footsteps of M. Scott Peck's
The Road Less Traveled, *Shawn Shea guides us down the road
to happiness in his insightful and engaging book. I found it
very compelling.*

—Jack Canfield
author, *Chicken Soup for the Soul*